BE STILL, AND KNOW THAT I AM GOD.

PSALM 46:10A

The Heart that Heals

BE STILL, AND KNOW THAT I AM GOD.
PSALM 46:10A

Healing Our Brokenness
Through the Promises of God

Patsy Burnette

FIRST PRINTING, 2019

ISBN 978-1-0818-7840-5

COVER DESIGN & INTERIOR ILLUSTRATION BY Blue Chair Blessing | www.bluechairblessing.com

AUTHOR PHOTO BY Katelyn King Photography | www.katelynkingphotography.com

Dedication

TO GINGER,

YOUR LIFE, AND SEEMINGLY UNTIMELY DEATH, HAS PROVEN TO
MANY THE UNQUESTIONABLE SOVEREIGNTY OF THE ALMIGHTY
GOD. YOUR BRIEF EXISTENCE ON EARTH WAS NOT IN VAIN, FOR
STILL TODAY, MANY ARE BEING TOUCHED BY ITS MESSAGE.
WHAT MAN INTENDED FOR EVIL, GOD HAS TURNED TO GOOD.

Thank you

To my father and mother, who exemplify a shining example of what it means to *Be still, and know that I am God* [Psalm 46:10a]. To my father who said I could do anything I put my mind to.

To husband and children, who are my support team and sounding boards. I love that I can depend on you to be there for me when I need it. I'm truly blessed to have you all in my life.

To my friends, Dinah Beck, Julie Clum, Sarah Liberty Hardee, Michelle Jarrell, Stephanie Little, Debbie Miller, Neva Parrott, Christine Rossiter, Jeremy Sweatt, and Bonnie Trimble, who have all in some way given life to this project.

To Micah and Alicia Hodges and Queen Bee Coffee Company for providing a creative and inspirational space to write in.

HOW TO GET THE MOST OUT OF THIS BOOK

This book is divided into three parts: the problem, the solution, and the application.

In PART ONE, we are going to look at how to breakdown the wall of emotions that so often plagues us as women. We'll also look at the emotional differences between us and our male counterparts. We will find out that we cannot do this alone—but you've probably already figured that out. Those are problems.

PART TWO is about casting our burdens on the Lord and bearing up others. Then there's a whole chapter where we learn about the God of all comfort. These are solutions.

Finally, in PART THREE, we will discuss growing in Christ. We'll take a look at what our response to burdens should be and the blessings of burdens. Yes, there are blessings! The book wraps up with some very practical applications that, I promise, will be a help to you. That's the application.

Just before each chapter, you'll find a coloring page with the key verse for that chapter. At the beginning of each chapter, there are some passages of Scripture to meditate on for the chapter. Do you like to meditate on Scripture as I do? We need to be rooted and grounded in the Word. We should write Scripture on our hearts, and the walls of our homes, and 3 x 5 cards, and Sticky Notes. . . . It's important! If your boyfriend or husband writes a love letter to you, how many times do you read it? Once? Twice? Over and over? This is God's love letter to us. Meditate on it. Be rooted and grounded in it. Write it on your heart!

At the end of each chapter, you're going to find a section designed specifically for that chapter— it's your homework, but in a good way. This section will encourage you to reflect on and apply what we've read. There is a space to write specific prayer requests, a passage of Scripture to meditate on, and a verse to memorize. I've also left you some room in the margins for notes. I don't know about you, but I love making notes when I'm reading a good book!

I freely interchange the words *burdens* and *brokenness*. You'll see this throughout the book.

Friend, I don't want you to think you are alone on this journey. You're not! Thousands of women who came before you have used these principles to heal their brokenness. You have not come here by accident. You have found this place, at this time, for a purpose. You are among friends!

Patsy

*Friendship is born at that moment when one person says to another:
What! You too? I thought I was the only one.* —C.S. Lewis

THIS BOOK BELONGS TO

_____

Please write your name here and own the journey!

Contents

Prologue

People have asked how I got to the point in my life where I could write a book like this. Because of that, and because I want you to fully understand where I am coming from when I write these things, I feel a brief explanation of my journey would be appropriate. This is how I learned to *Be still, and know that I am God* [Psalm 46:10a], and discovered the roots of the book, *The Heart That Heals*.

In December of 1987, I was a young wife and stay-at-home mother with two small children. My daughter, Rachel, was three years old, and my son, Philip Jr., was two. My parents and my younger sister, Ginger, had moved about three years prior from their home in Atlanta, Georgia, to the Tampa, Florida area where my father began a career in the restaurant business.

It was about two weeks before Christmas, my father's birthday, December 12. Ginger called me that evening from their home in Florida. She was eighteen years old at the time and had just graduated from high school the previous May. That afternoon, my parents gave Ginger her Christmas present, a brand-new computer, and she was so excited! She wanted to tell me all about it. My mom made a special dinner that evening for my father's birthday, and after dinner, Ginger told my dad that since it was his birthday, she would go and close up the restaurant where she and my parents worked. It wasn't uncommon for her to do that; she was one of the managers and a responsible, thoughtful daughter.

I received a phone call that night around midnight. It was a voice I knew well, but it sounded different. The two words that began that conversation, the only two words I remember from that conversation, I will never forget. They have echoed in my memory for all these years. They are words that put a lump in my throat and make my heart beat faster every time my mind rehearses them. The voice that night was my mother's, and the words were *Ginger's dead*.

That night changed our family forever. But not just our family, it changed forever the lives of many people who knew Ginger, and even many who didn't. The events of that evening are still touching lives today, years later. To paraphrase Genesis 50:20, what man intended for evil, God has turned to good.

When my mom taught art classes, she used to say *everything is fixable*. But that night, on the 12th of December, 1987, our family faced something that was not fixable. For the first time that I can remember, I was up against something I had no control over, something I wanted to fix, but couldn't. There was a hurt in my heart that I wanted to heal, but didn't know how. Until that night, I thought that this was something that happened to other people, not us, not Christians, not good people, not at Christmas time, not on my father's birthday. I wondered how a loving God could allow something like this to happen. There began the journey of *The Heart That Heals*.

My primary purpose in writing *The Heart that Heals* is not just to help you, although I hope this book is lifechanging for you! My ultimate desire though is that it will help you to help others. Your helping others will glorify God, and in turn it will also help you. Who receives the bigger blessing, the giver or the receiver? Human reasoning says the receiver. However, we all know the giver truly receives the biggest blessing of all. I want you to become the giver of encouragement. I want you to be an encourager!

I hope this book gives you the strength to cast your burdens on the Lord. But not just that, I hope it also gives you the tools you need to teach others how to do the same.

I attended a mission conference some years ago and watched as the keynote speaker demonstrated a very simple yet profound point. We'll call him Soulwinner 1. Soulwinner 1 stood on one side of the platform. Soulwinner 2, chosen from the audience, stood on the opposite side. Soulwinner 1 went out into the audience and brought back to his side one person representing a soul he had led to the Lord. Soulwinner 2 did the same. Soulwinner 1 then left that person, who represented the soul he had led to the Lord, and proceeded into the audience to retrieve another person representing yet another soul led to the Lord. He brought that person back to his side of the platform. At the same time, Soulwinner 2, who not only led a soul to the Lord but also taught that person to be a soul winner, went into the audience with the person he had led to the Lord. They both retrieved a person, brought them back to the platform, representing two more souls that were saved. Soulwinner 1 went out again, and the now four soul winners on the opposite side of the platform also went out. Now Soulwinner 1's side of the platform had three people and Soulwinner 2's side of the platform had eight. This continued for several minutes. Each time, Soulwinner 1 brought back one soul, and each time the soul winners on the opposite side of the platform doubled in number. Amazing concept! You can see now how quickly the one side filled with people representing souls won for Christ, and how slow, and toiling, the work continued on the keynote speaker's side of the platform.

Some years later, after viewing that demonstration, I realized that it not only applies to soulwinning [although it is vitally important and that is our purpose on this earth], but it pertains to many other areas of our lives as well.

I realized that the demonstration I had witnessed was similar to the old adage of teaching a hungry man to fish. The adage goes something like this: *If I feed a man a fish, I feed him for one day; but, if I teach him how to fish, I feed him for life.*

To draw a parallel between the demonstration, the old adage, and what I want to accomplish through *The Heart That Heals*, if I help you, I help only you; through Christ a life can be changed. However, if I help you help others, you help others to help others, and those others all help others to help others, then, through Christ many lives can be changed!

Do you see the difference between *a life* being changed and *lives* being changed? You can see how quickly teaching others to help others multiplies and how much more effective our work for God can be when we do that.

It's like being an encourager. I can be an encourager all day long and encourage one person at a time. But if I make encouragers, if I encourage you and then give you the tools to be an encourager, then there's two of us about the work of encouraging. Two encouragers, instead of one.

It's the same with burdens. I can show you how to cast your burden on the Lord all day long. But through this book, you become the one who can show someone else how to cast their burdens on Him.

So, my desire is that through Christ and with the help of *The Heart That Heals*, you will not only learn to cast your burdens on the Lord, but also be challenged and equipped with the tools to help others, which in turn will glorify God and help you.

Our choices have consequences. The pathway we walk has a destination. I want you to make good choices so that the consequences will be good. I want your destination to be one that glorifies God. If you're in a broken place, it may be difficult to make good choices. Is your pathway littered with the debris of brokenness? I want to help you get past all that and learn to be still, and know that He is God.

Write your name in the front of this book where it says *this book belongs to*. Own the journey. It's going to be lifechanging!

Part 1: THE PROBLEM

BE STILL, AND KNOW

THAT I AM GOD.

I WILL BE EXALTED

AMONG THE NATIONS,

I WILL BE EXALTED

IN THE EARTH!

PSALM 46:10

Chapter 1: THE EMOTIONAL WALL

Be still, and know that I am God.

I will be exalted among the nations,

I will be exalted in the earth! Psalm 46:10

SCRIPTURE TO MEDITATE ON
Proverbs 3:5, Hebrews 4:15a, 2 Corinthians 12:9 Write out one or more of these verses here.

If there were a key verse for *The Heart That Heals*, Psalm 46:10 would be it. If I had one single life verse, Psalm 46:10 would be that verse! But what does it mean to *Be still, and know that I am God*? How do we *be still*? How do we know God? It's not just enough to know that He is God; we need to know Him. How do we accomplish these things?

To *be still* means to relax, to let go, to abandon, to cease. To *know that I am God* means not only to know that He is God, but more importantly, to know His character. There needs to be a desire within us to love Him and everything about Him. He is the only true and living God.

Notes

Letting Go

In order for us to be able to *Be still, and know that I am God*, we are going to have to let go of and abandon all the emotional baggage that we carry. To do that, we must break down the wall of emotions that stands in the way of knowing God. That letting go, the total abandonment, that being still, that is how we are going to break down the wall of emotions that the burdens we are carrying have built up.

As we begin to *be still*, that wall of emotions begins to break down, and as that wall of emotions and brokenness begins to tumble, we begin to know God better. The more we know God, the more we are able to be still, and the more the wall tumbles. We must *Be still, and know that I am God* if we want to continue growing in Christ and keep our hearts in tune with His heart, as they should be.

What is Brokenness?

Brokenness can be caused by so many different things. It may be the death of a loved one as I, and possibly you, have experienced. It may be the inability to conceive a child, the loss of your health or the health of a loved one, a prodigal child, or dozens of other messy situations. Maybe your brokenness is caused by the loss of a job, financial problems, an abusive situation, guilt of past sins and worldly living, separation, divorce, hurtful actions or words, whether intentional or unintentional. I could go on and on naming things that may be the cause of brokenness. No doubt there are those of you reading this book and the particular situation that has caused your brokenness was not mentioned. You know what that situation is for you; the things that we will discuss pertain to your brokenness as well. Brokenness can be as big or bigger than the death of a loved one, or as small or smaller than unintentional hurtful words, and anything in between.

If you have ever worked in full or part time Christian service, you may have thought that when you began serving the Lord in that capacity, working with other Christians would be a perfect place—a place of love and peace where everyone said nice things to each other all the time and like the old song says *where never is heard a discouraging word.* It certainly should be and can be that way, but that's not always the way it works out. Possibly, at some point along the way, the perception you had of that *perfect workplace* was shattered. I've been there. I should have known it was not a perfect place to work. After all, I was there! How could I have ever thought it would be perfect, right?

Allow me to share my experience. Several years ago, at a mission conference hosted by our church, there was the début of a project that I had worked on for months. It was a special project, just for that conference. I remember how an opportunity arose for my own emotions to get in the way of my growing in Christ through unintentional, hurtful words.

The Lord had given me a desire to somehow display all of the missionaries our church supported on a wall near the church foyer. Our church had just recently moved to a new facility, and we did not have a representation of our missionaries anywhere, except for their names listed in the Sunday bulletin.

I spent months researching each of our more than forty missionaries. I gathered facts about their field, the country they served in, and the mission board they served under. I collected a map of each country that was represented and a photograph of each missionary family. I listed each family member's name and recorded detailed contact information for each missionary. Then I framed all of this information, the map, and photograph for each missionary in a beautiful glass document holder, one for each missionary.

The week leading up to the conference, a co-worker and I hung all forty plus displays around a lovely world map that hung in the hallway near the church foyer. I had worked so hard and was truly convinced I had done the best job I could do. I had seen a goal through to its end. Months of hard work had culminated into a beautiful and informative display for church members to enjoy and be informed about their missionaries.

The keynote speaker for the conference that year had no doubt seen bigger and better displays at other churches. He made comments during a service that the display we had was not sufficient in size, insignificant actually, and pretty much pointless. Those weren't his exact words, just a paraphrase. He thought we should have poster size displays for each missionary hung in a more prominent place. He had no idea that just a week prior, we had nothing at all to represent these servants of God, nothing except the Sunday bulletin. I thought we had taken a giant step forward from that, and we had.

When his comment rang out from the pulpit, I felt as if all the eyes in the auditorium were on me. I was not really hurt as much as I was embarrassed. Most of the people in the church probably did not even know that I was the person who had put that display together. Even my own father and mother, who were hosting the speaker and his wife in their home that week, didn't know. My co-workers knew though, and other people would eventually find out.

Now there was an opportunity in full bloom for me to build up a wall of emotions and allow my growth in Christ to be completely halted or slowed. Brokenness can be caused by something as little as unintentional, hurtful words, and that wall of emotions can spring up quickly, if we allow it to.

What Are Emotions?

We know what brokenness is, but let's talk a bit about emotions. Here is what Webster's dictionary says it is the *affective aspect of consciousness; a state of feeling; physical reactions such as anger or fear, subjectively experienced as strong feeling and physiologically involving changes that prepare the body for immediate, vigorous action.*

So, emotions affect conscious people— that's us; we are all conscious, aren't we? Emotions are a state of feeling that expresses itself physically; they cause a physical

Notes

reaction. They are subjective; they affect us all differently. They invoke strong feeling. They affect us physically to prepare the body for immediate and vigorous action. They certainly can change us for the good or for the bad.

I'm sure you have heard someone refer to the mind, will, and emotions, but have you ever thought of how closely related they are? What affects my emotions will affect my mind and the choices I make. What affects my emotions will affect my will and the actions I take. My emotions affect my whole self!

Basically, emotions are the way I feel. They are specific and intense and are a reaction to a particular event or series of events.

The connotation many times when one is speaking of emotions is that they are a bad thing. On the contrary! Emotions can be a bad thing or a good thing. Happy is an emotion. Joy is an emotion. There is nothing wrong with being happy or joyful, is there? But you don't meet people in therapy sessions for those types of emotions, do you? Those kinds of emotions are easily controlled. So, they're a good thing. However, emotions out of control are not a good thing. Out of control emotions is when I allow the way I feel to control me, instead of allowing what I know to be true to control me; that is never a good thing.

Emotions and My Understanding

Proverbs 3:5 says that I am not to lean on my understanding. *Trust in the Lord with all your heart, and do not lean on your own understanding.*

Lean not on my understanding because my understanding is very limited and finite. My limited, finite understanding is not reliable; I cannot rely on it. It is not trustworthy; I cannot trust it. I should not allow the way I feel to dictate what I do—my actions. I should only allow the truth to dictate my actions.

Remember the last wedding you attended? Does the couple stay married as long as they feel like they are in love? Or is love an action, a choice we make, something we do even when we don't feel like it? That couple that got married cannot allow the way they feel to dictate what they do. They cannot simply choose not to be married any longer the moment they don't feel in love anymore. If that were the case, probably none of us would be married, at least not for very long. And unfortunately, that is the view much of our society has taken today—I don't *feel* in love any longer, so we'll get a divorce. I cannot allow the way I feel to control the choices I make or the actions I take.

What Are Weaknesses?

What does God's Word say about emotions? Would you believe that the words *emotion* or *emotions* are not once mentioned in God's Word? However, the Bible does say in Hebrews 4:15a *For we do not have a High Priest Who is unable to sympathize with our weaknesses.*

What are our weaknesses? Weaknesses can be trials, weights, burdens and brokenness. In 2 Corinthians 12:9

Jesus says *My grace is sufficient for you, for My power is made perfect in weakness.* His power, His strength is made perfect in our weakness! His grace is sufficient for you and for me, and it is available!

Our weaknesses make us defenseless, powerless, and helpless—they are burdens. Brokenness could certainly be considered a weakness.

We Are All Different

There are different degrees of weaknesses and brokenness. Remember when we defined emotions? We read the word *subjectively*, which means that we are all affected differently—in different ways and to different degrees. What may devastate me emotionally might not affect you at all. And what may devastate you emotionally, might not affect me at all.

Let me Illustrate this. Do you like to garden? I care nothing about gardening. Oh, I appreciate a beautiful garden when I see one, don't get me wrong. But as for maintaining a garden of my own, I don't have the time nor desire to make the time or to do so. Our two wooded acres with some grass, lots of pine trees, shrubs and a small garden is enough for me. My mother-in-law, on the other hand, was an avid gardener. She and my father-in-law lived for years on the same five-acre piece of property. Over time they turned that once overgrown, wooded acreage into a beautifully manicured garden with strategically placed plants, flowers, trees, and shrubs.

I like technology. My husband bought me the latest and

greatest laptop for Christmas a few years ago. It had all the bells and whistles; it was fast, lightweight, top of the line, with a really big screen. I spent weeks transferring everything from my home computer and my work computer to this new and beautiful piece of machinery. I got it all set up like I wanted it. I was convinced this laptop would solve all of my problems, make my life easier, and help me work more efficiently, anywhere and everywhere.

Now, to bring this illustration to a close, my mother-in-law was really into her gardening; she didn't use a computer. I am really into computers; I don't garden. Most all of us have probably seen on television or possibly in person, the devastation a tornado can cause. If a tornado were to rip through my little two acres today, tearing up the grass, uprooting trees and shrubs, as long as it didn't hurt my family or me, besides being a little shaken up because I'm not too fond of tornados, I'd be alright.

On the other hand, if the same thing happened to my mother-in-law's beautiful five-acre manicured garden, she, I'm pretty sure, would have been devastated to lose what she and her husband had put so much of their time and energy into over many, many years.

Remember that new computer? Well, after days of transferring files, cleaning files off of the two old computers, loading new programs, deleting unwanted, pre-loaded programs, setting up everything just like I wanted it and thought it should be, the hard drive crashed! *Seriously*! A brand-new computer, the hard

Notes

Notes

drive crashed—an unrecoverable crash at that! To say the least, I was devastated! How could this happen? It was a brand-new computer! I had not backed up anything yet. A stupid mistake, I know, and I knew better at the time too. I was in shock! Years of work lost overnight. Needless to say, I'm better about backing up now.

Do you see how something that might devastate me emotionally might not affect you at all? And how something that might devastate you emotionally, might not affect me at all?

We are all affected emotionally in different ways, to differing degrees. I had a co-worker once who cried at the drop of a hat. I've probably cried twice in the last twenty years. We are all different and affected differently. We can even be affected differently by the same brokenness or burden.

As women [If you are a man reading this book, I apologize. I expected you to be a woman, but that's ok, just keep reading], I believe we have a special ability to perceive in others the presence of brokenness and burdens. I believe also that we have a special ability within ourselves to feel brokenness and burdens. These abilities can be a help or a hindrance to us when it comes to breaking down the wall of emotions.

One thing we must realize is that our ability to perceive and feel brokenness and burdens is unique to us as women. Men are created differently. In the next chapter, we will look at the emotional differences between us and our male counterparts.

REFLECTION & APPLICATION

1. What did God teach me through this chapter?
2. How can I obediently respond to what I've learned?
3. What steps of faith does God want me to take now?

PRAYER & PETITIONS *Confession, Gratitude, Praise, and Requests*

MEDITATION & MEMORIZATION
Meditate on Psalm 46. Write out and memorize verse 10.

WHEN YOU PASS THROUGH THE WATERS, I WILL BE WITH YOU;

AND THROUGH THE RIVERS, THEY SHALL NOT OVERWHELM YOU;

WHEN YOU WALK THROUGH FIRE YOU SHALL NOT BE BURNED,

AND THE FLAME SHALL NOT CONSUME YOU.

ISAIAH 43:2

Chapter 2: THE EMOTIONAL DIFFERENCE

When you pass through the waters, I will be with you;

and through the rivers, they shall not overwhelm you;

when you walk through fire you shall not be burned,

and the flame shall not consume you. Isaiah 43:2

SCRIPTURE TO MEDITATE ON
Genesis 2:23, Job 34:19, Mark 12:17 Write out one or more of these verses here.

There is an emotional difference between a man and a woman. I probably didn't have to tell you that. More than likely, you'd already made this discovery. So why have I dedicated an entire chapter to it? I want to encourage you, as the unique creature you are, and who was created by a loving and all-knowing God, to be the helper He intended for you to be. This is where the helper meets the burden bearer. He created you the way you are for a purpose.

We as women have the ability within ourselves to perceive and feel brokenness and burdens that men may not perceive, feel, or even begin to comprehend. There are so many jokes about trying to understand women, and there's a reason why—God made us different, on purpose!

Why Are We Different?

Women feel with the right side of their brain, which invokes a sense of empathy. Men feel with the left side of their brain, which tries to find a solution.

Why are we like that? Why are men and women so different from each other? Because God made us that way. He made us as women different from men for a unique purpose. He also made us as women different from each other—we found that out in the last chapter.

Remember how we discussed the fact that emotions are subjective, which means they affect us all in different ways? God created us for His glory and for His purpose, and He created us differently from the male species and from each other for a reason. We're unique! In a good way.

Burden Bearers and Helpers

Men are made to be burden bearers. Women are not. We are created to be helpers. We find a few examples in the Bible of women bearing burdens. However, the Bible mostly talks of donkeys, Israelites, Egyptians, Hebrews, men, sons, and servants bearing burdens. Women are not emotionally designed or equipped to bear burdens. We are designed, by God, to be helpers. That is one reason it is so important for us to give our burdens to the Lord.

In Genesis 2:18, God essentially says *Adam, you need help*! God knew, when He created Adam, that he [Adam] would need a helper. It was no surprise to God at all. God also knew that although He had created all kinds of animals, none of them would be a suitable helper for Adam. He had not yet created the helper that Adam needed.

Verse 18 goes on to say *Then the LORD God said, It is not good that the man should be alone; I will make him a helper fit for him.* Adam needed a helper that was *fit for him*, and he had not found that among all the animals that God had created.

I find it humorous, though, that first, before God makes a helper for Adam, He gives Adam the job of naming all the animals He created. Do you think God knew that if He were to wait until after Eve were created to have Adam name all the animals, Adam would have been so enamored with Eve that the job might not ever get done—I wonder?

So, in Genesis 2:20, we find Adam giving names to all the animals. Adam must have also, at that time, been looking for a mate of his own. We would assume that he would have noticed that the animals all had mates. Adam must have realized that the elephant had a companion, that the lion and tiger had their own lioness and tigress, that the sea gull had a cohort, and the cockatoo had a pal.

All the animals that God created had mates. But the Bible says that there was not a mate found for Adam. I guess that the dog really isn't man's best friend after all. Verse 20 says *The man gave names to all livestock, and to the birds of the heavens, and to every beast of the field* [these are natural born burden bearers]. *But for Adam there was not found a helper for him.*

Notes

Notes

God creates for Adam a mate, a helper, in Genesis 2:22-23. Verse 22 says *And the rib that the Lord God had taken from the man He made into a woman and brought her to the man.* I would love to have been there to see that! Can you just imagine the look on Adam's face when Eve came walking out from around that bush or from behind that tree? A perfect woman; probably the way we all would like to look, with a perfect figure, perfect skin, and perfect hair. Oh, how I would like to have seen his face! Can you imagine how Adam must have felt after naming all those animals, seeking but not finding, looking to no avail for a mate. Finally, there was Eve, the creation of an Almighty God to purposely be a helper to the first man after God's own heart. What a moment!

The passage goes on to say in verse 23 *Then the man said, This at last is bone of my bones and flesh of my flesh.* Doesn't that just sound like a beautiful love song? *Bone of my bones and flesh of my flesh.* Then Adam gives her a name, *she shall be called Woman, because she was taken out of Man.*

God knew all along that He would create a helper for Adam. It was no surprise to Him that *for Adam there was not found a helper fit for him* [Geneses 2:20]. It was no surprise to God that Adam needed a helper. God intended it to be that way. Woman, the man's helper, was taken out of man. I'd like to think since God took woman out of man, that now man is missing something that woman completes in him. Have you ever thought of it that way? There is something in me, the helper, which completes my husband, the burden bearer.

Designed Different on Purpose

As women, God made us special. We are purposely designed with a different emotional makeup than a man. Why do you think God made a woman for Adam instead of just creating another Adam for Adam? He created a woman for Adam because Adam needed something different than himself. Men and women are different because God made us that way for a unique purpose.

Several years ago, my father and mother were involved in a serious automobile accident. They were attempting to exit a very busy highway just outside the city of Atlanta. The exit ramp was backed up with cars waiting in the emergency lane to exit the highway. My father and mother were sitting still in their car, waiting to exit, when they were rear-ended by a car going highway speed. Their car was totaled.

My father, who amazingly was not badly injured, called me from the emergency room and this is what he said: *Your mother and I have been in a car accident. If you want to see your mother, you'd better come.*

You can imagine the panic that gripped my heart, the lump that formed in my throat, and the knot that formed in my stomach. All the way to the hospital I prayed, *Lord, just let me see my mother alive one more time—please, let me tell her how much I love her, just one more time.* I may have even cried.

When I arrived at the hospital, I found my father pacing the floor of the emergency room and my mother in x-ray. She was in a great deal of pain and spent months in

Notes

therapy following the accident, but her injuries were not life threatening. To say the least, I was very thankful and quite relieved!

My father said, *if you want to see your mother, you'd better come*. That's simple enough. But me, being the emotional creature that I am, read between the lines and added some words like *alive* and *now*. Maybe I should say my emotions added these words.

Who is in control here, my emotions or me? You may be feeling the same thing right now in your own life. You may be asking yourself, *who is in control, my emotions or me?*

There is a huge emotional difference between men and women. However, even though there is this great difference, we were both created by God, and He made us both for His glory and for a unique purpose.

The Work of His Hands

Isaiah 43:1-7 is a beautiful passage in which the Lord speaks to Jacob, to Israel, and to all of us. In this passage He is reminding us that He created and formed us, that we are not to fear because He has redeemed and called us by name, and that we are His! The passage says in Verses 2-3: *When you pass through the waters, I will be with you; and through the rivers, they shall not overwhelm you; when you walk through fire you shall not be burned, and the flame shall not consume you. For I am the Lord your God, the Holy One of Israel, your Savior.* What a beautiful reminder of His sovereignty!

Are you passing though the deep and treacherous waters today? He is with you. Are you swimming through the swift flowing rivers of life, just barely keeping your head above the waters? He promises that they shall not overwhelm you. Are you walking through fiery trials? *You shall not be burned, and the flame shall not consume you*, He says. Why? *For I am the LORD your God, the Holy One of Israel, your Savior.* Oh, how wonderful to have a God like that! A Savior! The Holy One!

The passage goes on to say in verses 4-5 that we are precious in His sight, that He loves us, and that we should not fear for He is with us. Why? Verse 7 is the why: because we are called by His name and created for His glory. He has created us, formed us, and made us [both male and female, both non-emotional and emotional] for His honor, for His glory, and for a unique purpose.

Two of my favorite passages in the Bible are about the potter and the clay. One is found in Jeremiah, the other in Isaiah 64:8, where it says *But now, O Lord, You are our Father; we are the clay, and You are our Potter; we are all the work of Your hand.* God created us for His unique purpose and we are all the work of His hands. Do you ever think of yourself as the work of God's hands? He knows us just as the potter knows his lump of clay. What a precious thought! Your mind, your will, and your emotions, are all the work of His Hands.

Job 34:19 reminds us that God is not a regarder of persons; the rich and the poor are all the same to Him, *for they are all the work of His hands.*

Notes

Made in His Image

We are made in His image. In Mark 12:14, a group of Pharisees and Herodians came to Jesus and asked Him this question, *Teacher, we know that You are true and do not care about anyone's opinion. For You are not swayed by appearances, but truly teach the way of God. Is it lawful to pay taxes to Caesar, or not?* Jesus asked them to bring Him a coin. And then in verse 16 He asks, *Whose likeness and inscription is this?* They answered, *Caesar's.* Then Jesus said to them in verse 17, *Render to Caesar the things that are Caesar's, and to God the things that are God's.* The image of Caesar was stamped on the coin that the Pharisees and Herodians brought to Jesus. Whose image is stamped on us?

I love the old hymn *O To Be Like Thee* by Thomas Chisholm. The refrain goes like this:

> *O to be like Thee! O to be like Thee!*
> *Blessed Redeemer, pure as Thou art;*
> *Come in Thy sweetness, come in Thy fullness;*
> *Stamp Thine own image deep on my heart.*

We are made in the image and likeness of God. We belong to Him. We should render ourselves to Him just as the coin with Caesar's image was to be rendered to Caesar. We also read this account in Luke 20, *render to Caesar the things that are Caesar's, and to God the things that are God's.* I've always felt when passages like this were repeated in different parts of the Bible, that it only goes to emphasize their importance. Have you rendered yourself to God?

So far, we've seen that we are emotionally different from each other and that we are emotionally different from men. We've learned that we are not made to be burden bearers, but instead we are made to be helpers. We know that God made us the way He did for His honor, for His glory, and for a unique purpose. And, we learned that we are made in His image and we should therefore render ourselves unto Him.

So, when burdens become a part of our lives, when brokenness takes over, when we need to break down that wall of emotions, we must recognize that we cannot do this alone. We'll look at that in the next chapter.

REFLECTION & APPLICATION

1. What did God teach me through this chapter?
2. How can I obediently respond to what I've learned?
3. What steps of faith does God want me to take now?

PRAYER & PETITIONS *Confession, Gratitude, Praise, and Requests*

MEDITATION & MEMORIZATION
Meditate on Isaiah 43:1-7. Write out and memorize verse 2

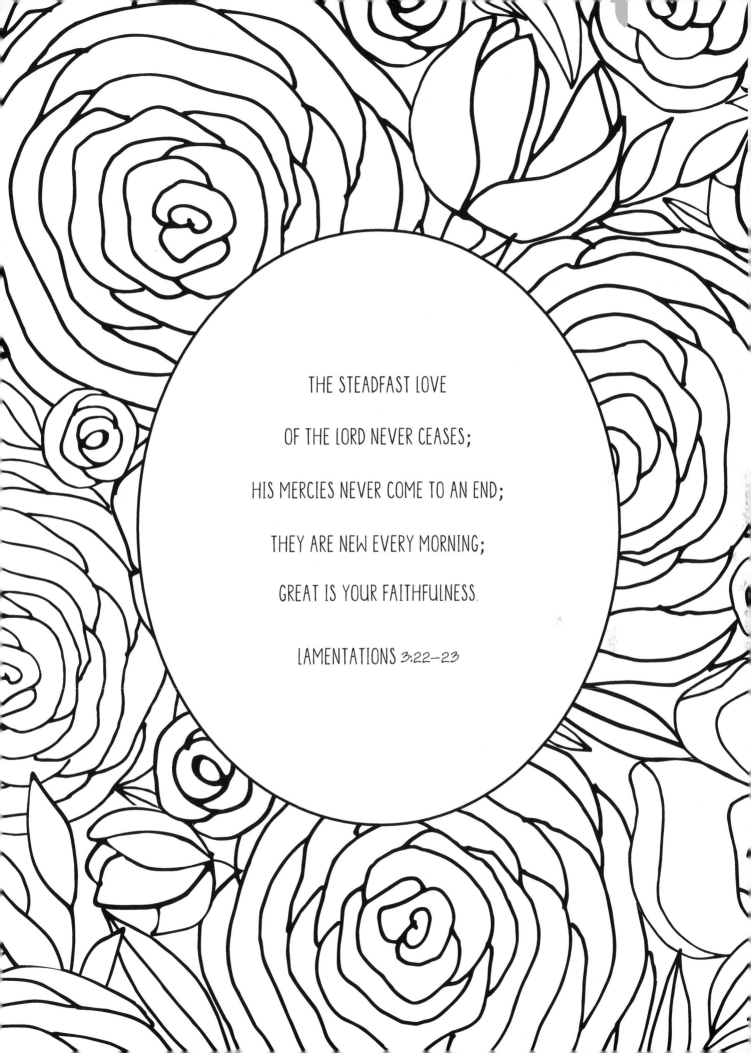

THE STEADFAST LOVE

OF THE LORD NEVER CEASES;

HIS MERCIES NEVER COME TO AN END;

THEY ARE NEW EVERY MORNING;

GREAT IS YOUR FAITHFULNESS.

LAMENTATIONS 3:22-23

Chapter 3: WE CANNOT DO THIS ALONE

The steadfast love of the Lord never ceases;

His mercies never come to an end; they are new every morning;

great is your faithfulness. Lamentations 3:22-23

SCRIPTURE TO MEDITATE ON

Isaiah 53:3a, Jeremiah 1:6, Philippians 4:13 Write out one or more of these verses here.

In Jeremiah 1:6, we find Jeremiah speaking to the Lord. Jeremiah says *Then I said, Ah, Lord God! Behold, I do not know how to speak, for I am only a youth.* Jeremiah would have been about 21 years old at the time. I find it somewhat humorous the way he speaks God. *Ah, Lord God! Behold,* he says, as if he were going to reveal something new to God, something God didn't already know.

Jeremiah says *I do not know how to speak, for I am only a youth.* Jeremiah realized that he could not do alone what God had called him to do. He realized the he needed God's help. So, he went to the Helper!

Notes

He is Our Hope

God never asks us to do anything or go through anything that He will not empower us to do or give us the grace to endure. Sometimes we forget that, and we must remind ourselves that we cannot handle things on our own, and that we need help from God. But that's ok, because that is what God wants. He wants people who are able to recognize and admit that they cannot do it alone. He wants people who want His help and acknowledge that they need His help. God can do more through a person who realizes that they cannot do it without His help than He can through a person [no matter how diligent they are] who thinks they can handle life on their own!

We read in Philippians 4:13 *I can do all things* [even heal my heart from brokenness] *through Him Who strengthens me.* We all need His help. We all need His strength. All the works of His hands need His help and His strength. Aren't you so glad it's available? I am! All we have to do is acknowledge that we cannot do it in our own strength and quit trying to do it in our own strength!

Moses, like Jeremiah, said that he could not do what God called him to do without help from God. So, God sent Aaron to help Moses. God uses people who cannot do it alone. He uses the weak, the broken, the people in need like you and me.

We cannot do this alone. He is our only hope!
Lamentations 3:21-26 says *But this I call to mind, and therefore I have hope: The steadfast love of the Lord never ceases; His mercies never come to an end; they are new every morning; great is Your faithfulness. The Lord is my*

portion, says my soul, therefore, I will hope in Him. The Lord is good to those who wait for Him, to the soul who seeks Him. It is good that one should wait quietly for the salvation of the Lord. His compassions fail not. His mercies are new every single morning!

I remember after my sister's death, when I finally got to the point where I was able to sleep again at night, that I would wake up in the morning to the realization of her death, and it would hit me all over again. It was not a dream, not a nightmare. It was real! It had really happened!

That is when I claimed this passage, *Therefore, I will hope in Him...* His compassions fail not. His mercies are new every single morning!

He is our only hope, and only by His grace are we able to make it through. In 1 Corinthians 15:10, Paul says *But by the grace of God I am what I am, and His grace toward me* [put your name here] *was not in vain. On the contrary, I worked harder than any of them, though it was not I* [put your name here too]*, but the grace of God that is with me.* He has bestowed on me His grace, and that is what gets me through this brokenness in my heart. It's what makes me able to endure. Now, it is my job to make sure that His grace is not bestowed on me in vain. Paul says *I worked harder than any of them* [but not alone]*, though it was not I, but the grace of God that is with me.* He is our only hope and only by His grace can we endure. Only by His grace can I cast my burden. Only by His grace can I bear the burdens of others. We cannot do it alone, but we can do it by His grace.

Notes

Notes

Trusting God

Romans 8:28 says *And we know that for those who love God all things work together for good, for those who are called according to His purpose.* If we turn this around and paraphrase it a bit, to make it a little easier to understand, it would say, *those who love God know that all things work together for good.*

When I read this, I have to ask myself if that knowing *for those who love God all things work together for good,* controls me? Or, do I allow my emotions to control me? Do I trust God enough to let the *knowing* control me? And what about the part that says *for those who love God?* Do I really love God enough to trust Him?

We do not easily trust those that we do not properly love. Do I really love God that much? Do I love Him enough to trust Him?

I find it takes a good amount of faith to trust Him. I've also found that when I step out by faith and trust, my love for Him grows. When my love for Him grows, so grows my trust in Him, and I more readily place my trust in Him as I see His goodness.

At first, it may be difficult for us to cast our burdens on Him because there may be a limited amount of trust. But as we begin to cast our burdens, we grow in the knowledge of our Lord and Savior Jesus Christ as it says in 2 Peter 3:18, *But grow in the grace and knowledge of our Lord and Savior Jesus Christ.* Along with growing in grace and in knowledge, we also grow in love for Him.

As a result, we are able to place more trust in Him. It

becomes easier for us to cast our burdens. We trust more. Then we love more, then we trust more, love more, trust more, love, trust. . . . It is through this process that we really learn to love God wholly, and to trust Him fully. The result is the knowledge we gain of His faithfulness to work out all things for our good and for His glory.

I think it is quite possible that this verse, Romans 8:28, may not always be used in its proper context. *And we know that for those who love God all things work together for good, for those who are called according to His purpose.* It seems cold and uncaring if we flippantly say *all things work together for good* to someone who is hurting in their brokenness.

Many times, we may quote the middle part of the verse and forget about the first and last parts that say: *for those who love God . . . for those who are called according to His purpose.*

Loving God and being called according to His purpose, those are the most important parts of this verse. If we have those things right in our lives, then we can be assured that *all things* [will] *work together for good.*

Most all of us, at one time or another, have watched children participate in a three-legged relay race. In case you haven't seen it in action or have forgotten what it is like, I'll refresh your memory. Each team is made up of two individuals. One leg of each person is tied together. The race usually goes along fairly well, as long as the two people, whose legs are tied together, keep their rhythm and are going the same direction with the same goal and purpose.

Some time ago I witnessed such a race in which four teams participated. The race was run around a circle with four cones that were equally spaced along the circle and one cone in the center of the circle. Each team started at a certain cone, had to complete a certain number of laps around the circle, pass their starting cone and go to the center of the circle to grab the winning cone. In this particular race, one of the rules was that if you tag the opponent in front of you, they are disqualified. As I watched in amazement, wondering how any two people could be so coordinated to pull this off, the team that was leading was rounding the last cone. They had only to round that cone, head for the middle, and pick up the winning cone. However, I could see that something was terribly wrong. The girl on the right had her eyes set on the team in front of them. She was reaching and could almost tag them—her goal was to tag and disqualify that team. At the same time though, the girl on the left had her eyes set on the winning cone. She was headed to victory—her goal was to grab the winning cone and win the race. Because they did not have the same goal or purpose, they sadly, even though they were leading, lost the race.

Do you really love God? Are you living your life according to His purpose? Do you and God have the same goals and purpose, or are you and God like the two girls who lost the three-legged race with different goals and a different purpose?

For Our Good and His Glory

God works out all things for our good. However, that does not mean that all things that happen to us are going to be good things. There is still evil present in this fallen world, and we are still a part of that.

Late on a cold, December night, down a long, straight, narrow, Florida highway, my sister Ginger was headed home from work. Headed in the opposite direction was a man in a large, heavy, work truck. He was headed home from a bar. His headlights danced into my sister's lane. As they came closer and closer, approaching rapidly, she chose to leave the highway and pulled her car onto the shoulder of the road. She hung onto the steering wheel, maneuvering the car on the rough shoulder of the road. He pulled his big truck onto the same shoulder and did the same. Her last words were frantic screams of *what do I do now, what do I do now*? The two vehicles met head on, and my sister was immediately ushered in the arms of a loving, Almighty, all-knowing, compassionate God.

Yes, there is evil in this present world, and we are not going to be able to escape being a part of that evil just because we are Christians. But we have the assurance that the One Who created this world [not in its present condition] is the same One Who has overcome this world. And He is able to turn that evil around for our good and for His glory.

Do you really love God? Do you have your mind set on His purpose and His goal for your life? Remember, we were created for His glory.

Notes

Notes

Does Jesus Care?

Have you ever wondered, *Does Jesus really care? Does He really care about me?* Let me assure you, friend, He does! I came across this old song that says it better than I ever could.

Does Jesus Care?

Does Jesus care when my heart is pained
Too deeply for mirth and song;
As the burdens press, and the cares distress,
And the way grows weary and long?

Does Jesus care when my way is dark
With a nameless dread and fear?
As the daylight fades into deep night shades,
Does He care enough to be near?

Does Jesus care when I've tried and failed
To resist some temptation strong;
When for my deep grief I find no relief,
Though my tears flow all the night long?

Does Jesus care when I've said goodbye
To the dearest on earth to me,
And my sad heart aches till
It nearly breaks is it aught to Him? Does He see?

O yes, He cares — I know He cares!
His heart is touched with my grief
When the days are weary, the long nights dreary,
I know my Savior cares.

John W. Peterson. Great Hymns of the Faith. Grand Rapids, MI: Singspiration Music, a division of Zondervan Corporation; 1974. p. 289 words by Frank E. Graeff, 1860-1919

Of course, He cares! Isaiah 53:3a says *He was despised and rejected by men, a man of sorrows and acquainted with grief.* Jesus was a man of sorrows, acquainted with grief during His earthly ministry. He was acquainted with the grief of others and also His own grief on the cross of Calvary. And yes, He is acquainted with your grief too! He cares for you!

There is another song that says *When you can't see His hand, trust His heart.* There have been many times when I could not see His hand, and I had to just trust His heart. You may be in a situation like that today. You may be in a difficult place where you can't see His hand and can't understand the *why* of what you are going through. Can you trust His heart? Because you know, you can't do this alone.

We've looked at the problem: The emotional wall, the emotional difference, and how we cannot do this alone. Now, let's look at the solution! Part two is next, and it's all about casting our burdens on the Lord and bearing up others. Then, there's a whole chapter where we learn about the God of all comfort. This is the cream of *The Heart That Heals*! It's the good stuff. Don't skip it!

notes

REFLECTION & APPLICATION

1. What did God teach me through this chapter?
2. How can I obediently respond to what I've learned?
3. What steps of faith does God want me to take now?

PRAYER & PETITIONS *Confession, Gratitude, Praise, and Requests*

MEDITATION & MEMORIZATION
Meditate on Lamentations 3:21-26. Write out and memorize verses 22-23.

Part 2: THE SOLUTION

CAST YOUR BURDEN ON THE LORD,

AND HE WILL SUSTAIN YOU;

HE WILL NEVER PERMIT

THE RIGHTEOUS TO BE MOVED.

PSALM 55:22

Chapter 4: CASTING OUR BURDENS

Cast your burden on the Lord, and He will sustain you;
He will never permit the righteous to be moved. Psalm 55:22

SCRIPTURE TO MEDITATE ON

Proverbs 3:5, Nehemiah 9:21, Psalm 55:22 Write out one or more of these verses here.

We read in Psalm 55:22 that we are to cast our burden upon the Lord. But how exactly do we do that? One way we cast our burdens and learn to trust Him is through prayer. I heard someone say once, and you may have heard this too, *never let your troubles get you down, except down on your knees*. Isn't that just so true!

The Bible assures us that not only will our prayers be heard but that they also will be answered. One of my favorite passages of Scripture [you may have noticed I have many favorite passages] is found in Isaiah 65:24 where it says *Before they call I will answer; while they are yet speaking, I will hear*. What a promise! Can you imagine a God Who answers before we call and while we are still speaking? How can we not trust a God like that?

Casting Burdens Requires Humility

What an awesome God we serve! A God Who answers before we call and before we are even done speaking. A God Who wants us to cast all of our burdens and care on Him. A God Who cares for me even though I fail Him so very often.

1 Peter 5:7 says *Casting all your anxieties on Him, because He cares for you*. If we hesitate in casting our anxiety on Him, aren't we essentially saying, *Lord, I can handle this on my own, I don't need you in my life*? Or, could we be saying, *Lord, I don't trust you to handle this like I think it needs to be handled*?

Do we really think that we can handle our brokenness on our own and that we don't need Him? No, down deep in our souls I believe we know we need Him. But it requires a certain amount of humility on our part to recognize the fact that we can't do this on our own. It requires humility to admit that we need God's help. It requires a humble spirit to place our trust in Him. But we must trust Him fully, with every part of our lives. Not just the big stuff, but the small stuff too.

As women, whether we're single, married, mothers, grandmothers, sisters, stay-at-home moms, full-time employees, or whatever we are in our daily lives, there are so many burdens that we try to bear. I am convinced we were never meant to bear these burdens. One reason we bear them alone is because we are not casting them upon the Lord. We're holding on to them, but why?

Proverbs 3:5-6 says *Trust in the Lord with all your heart*, *and do not lean on your own understanding. In all your ways acknowledge Him, and He will make straight your paths.* He will make straight my path, even through trials and tribulation, and even through the brokenness and the messiness. He wants to guide me, but for that to happen I must allow Him to make straight my path. I must cast my burdens and not continue to hold on to them.

Casting Burdens Requires Trust

Casting our burdens on the Lord requires a significant amount of trust in Him. The Bible gives us some very specific promises regarding trust.

Blessed are all who take refuge in Him [Psalm 2:12b].

But let all who take refuge in You rejoice; let them ever sing for joy, and spread Your protection over them, that those who love Your name may exult in You [Psalm 5:11].

And those who know Your name put their trust in You, for You, O Lord, have not forsaken those who seek You [Psalm 9:10].

Wondrously show Your steadfast love, O Savior of those who seek refuge from their adversaries at Your right hand [Psalm 17:7].

The Lord is my rock and my fortress and my deliverer, my God, my rock, in Whom I take refuge, my shield, and the horn of my salvation, my stronghold [Psalm 18:2].

notes

Notes

This God—His way is perfect; the Word of the Lord proves true; He is a shield for all those who take refuge in Him [Psalm 18:30].

Oh, how abundant is Your goodness, which You have stored up for those who fear You and worked for those who take refuge in You, in the sight of the children of mankind [Psalm 31:19].

The Lord redeems the life of His servants; none of those who take refuge in Him will be condemned [Psalm 34:22].

Trust in the Lord, and do good; dwell in the land and befriend faithfulness. . . . Commit your way to the Lord; trust in Him, and He will act [Psalm 37:3-5].

The Lord helps them and delivers them; He delivers them from the wicked and saves them, because they take refuge in Him [Psalm 37:40].

Blessed is the man who makes the Lord his trust, who does not turn to the proud, to those who go astray after a lie [Psalm 40:4].

Trust in Him at all times, O people; pour out your heart before Him; God is a refuge for us [Psalm 62:8].

Let the righteous one rejoice in the Lord and take refuge in Him! Let all the upright in heart exult [Psalm 64:10].

For you, O Lord, are my hope, my trust, O Lord, from my youth [Psalm 71:5].

But for me it is good to be near God; I have made the Lord God my refuge, that I may tell of all Your works [Psalm 73:28].

I will say to the Lord, My refuge and my fortress, my God, in Whom I trust. . . . He will cover you with His pinions [feathers], *and under His wings you will find refuge; His faithfulness is a shield and buckler* [Psalm 91:2-4].

O Israel, trust in the Lord! He is their help and their shield. O house of Aaron, trust in the Lord! He is their help and their shield. You who fear the Lord, trust in the Lord! He is their help and their shield [Psalm 115:9-11].

It is better to take refuge in the Lord than to trust in man. It is better to take refuge in the Lord than to trust in princes [Psalm 118: 8-9].

Those who trust in the Lord are like Mount Zion, which cannot be moved, but abides forever [Psalm 125:1].

He is my steadfast love and my fortress, my stronghold and my deliverer, my shield and He in Whom I take refuge, Who subdues peoples under me [Psalm 144:2].

In the book of Psalms alone, we find over twenty-two verses that contain promises for those who will put their trust in the Lord. Can you trust Him today? Can you trust Him enough to cast your burden? He cares for you!

He Will Sustain You

I find that one reason I hold onto my burden is because I think that I can handle it. I cannot! Psalm 55:22 says *Cast your burden on the Lord, and He will sustain you; He will never permit the righteous to be moved.* He will sustain me! It doesn't say here that He *might* sustain me; it says He *will* sustain me! He promises—He will sustain me!

What does it mean to sustain? To sustain means to give support, to uphold, and to give relief. The word *sustain* is used only four times in the Bible. All four are found in the Old Testament.

We find one of those time here in Nehemiah 9:21, where it says *Forty years You sustained them in the wilderness, and they lacked nothing. Their clothes did not wear out and their feet did not swell.* God led the Israelites through the wilderness for forty years! Their clothes never wore out, their shoes never wore out, and their feet were never swollen. And if that's not enough, the Bible says *they lacked nothing*! For forty years they lacked absolutely nothing at all! God knew and met all of their needs corporately and individually. He sustained over one million Israelites wandering through the wilderness for forty years. Don't you think He can sustain you, and me too?

God wants to sustain us. He wants to give us support. He wants to uphold us, and He wants to give us relief. He says so in His Word. All we have to do is to give Him our burdens. All you have to do is to cast your burden and *He will sustain you*. He promises!

Cast Your Burden and Leave it There

How many times have you cast your burdens to the Lord only to take them back again? You pray. You give your burden to the Lord, and then you call your friend Sally and say *Sally, I just don't know what I'm going to do . . . blah, blah, blah, blah, blah, blah, blah. . . .* There you go again. You've retrieved your burden from the Lord, and now you're trying to bear it again, by yourself. Or, did you ever, really cast your burden in the first place?

The word *cast* used in Psalm 55:22 means to throw off, to get rid of, to discard, or to shed. It means to completely let go of with no intention of ever taking it back. It has no connotation of retrieving that which was cast.

How often do we retrieve that which was cast? How often do we temporarily cast our burden on the Lord just to see what He will do? We know it's temporary. We never intended for it to be permanent, unless He does what we think He should do. How often do we take our burdens back because we don't see God working? Or, because we suddenly decide we can handle it on our own, or we can do something to take care of it and we don't need His help? Maybe we see Him working, but don't like His method?

When you voted in the last presidential election, you went to the polls and you *cast* your ballot. Did you expect to retrieve it again if the results didn't turn out the way you thought they should? No, of course not. Your intention was to cast your ballot once and be done with it. In that same way we should cast our burdens on the Lord. Cast them and be done. Don't take them back!

Cast your burden on the LORD, and don't take it back. He wants to sustain you!

Psalm 34:8 says *Oh, taste and see that the Lord is good! Blessed is the man* [or woman] *who takes refuge in Him!*

Do you trust Him? Do you trust Him enough to cast your burden upon Him? He wants to sustain you!

Fear is a Burden

Job said in Job 3:25 *For the thing that I fear comes upon me, and what I dread befalls me*. Are you fearful? Is there something you are dreading? Maybe it's the fear or dread of not being a good wife or mother.

Maybe you live in fear of financial hardship or losing your health. Do you wrestle with the fear of losing someone you love— maybe it's a parent, a spouse or a child? Have fear and dread taken over your life? Fear is a burden. 2 Timothy 1:7 says *For God gave us a spirit not of fear but of power and love and self-control.*

If God did not give us a spirit of fear, where did it come from? It comes from Satan. He doesn't want us to trust in God. He would much rather we be fearful. Satan uses our old sinful self to place doubts and fears in our minds. 1 Peter 5:8 reminds us that just as a lion attacks the sick, young, or straggling animal and chooses victims who are alone or not alert, our adversary, the devil, is waiting and ready to attack us when we are struggling and weak. The verse reads *Be sober-minded; be watchful. Your adversary the devil prowls around like a roaring lion, seeking someone to devour.*

He is ready, waiting, and eager to devour any Christian who is feeling alone, weak, and helpless. Sometimes we are so focused on our troubles that we forget to watch for his attacks. It's at these time that we are most vulnerable. Keep your guard up! Be sober-minded and be watchful.

Fear is a burden we need to cast upon the Lord. We need to be sober, be always watching, be vigilant, and constantly keeping our eyes on the Lord. Psalm 56:3 says *When I am afraid, I put my trust in You.* Cast your burdens, your brokenness and your fears on the Lord, and trust in Him today!

Every opportunity for fear is an equal opportunity for faith. If your circumstance brings you face to face with fear, you're also standing face to face with the option of choosing faith instead. Choose faith! Desperate situations are often divine setups for the miraculous. —Caroline Harrington

In this chapter we've talked about casting our burdens on the Lord. In the next chapter, we'll discuss bearing up others and their burdens. Both of these actions require strength. We just have to remember it is in *His* strength that we are able to do these things, not our own.

Notes

REFLECTION & APPLICATION

1. What did God teach me through this chapter?
2. How can I obediently respond to what I've learned?
3. What steps of faith does God want me to take now?

PRAYER & PETITIONS *Confession, Gratitude, Praise, and Requests*

MEDITATION & MEMORIZATION
Meditate on Psalm 55. Write out and memorize verse 22.

AND LET US NOT GROW WEARY

OF DOING GOOD,

FOR IN DUE SEASON

WE WILL REAP,

IF WE DO NOT GIVE UP.

GALATIANS 6:9

Chapter 5: BEARING UP OTHERS

And let us not grow weary of doing good,

for in due season we will reap,

if we do not give up. Galatians 6:9

SCRIPTURE TO MEDITATE ON
John 13:34, Galatians 6:2, James 5:16b Write out one or more of these verses here.

Galatians 6:2 says that we are to *bear one another's burdens*. The word used in this verse for *burdens* refers to the temporary overload that a friend may carry. This word is distinctly different from the word used in verse five of the same chapter which says *each will have to bear his own load.* The word used in verse five, often translated *burdens*, refers to the everyday load that we or a friend may bear. Two verses, Galatians 6:2 and Galatians 6:5, one word—*burdens*. Two different meanings. The first is a temporary overload. The second is an everyday load.

Bearing up others requires us to come alongside the overburdened one and help by bearing up their temporary overload.

Praying for Others

In the last chapter, we looked at prayer as a way of casting our burdens. But did you know that prayer is also a way to bear the burdens of others?

We read in James 5:16 that we are to *pray for one another, that you may be healed. The prayer of a righteous person has great power as it is working.*

In some translations of the Bible, this verse talks of *effectual fervent prayer.* What does that mean? The word *effectual* means *producing or able to produce a desired outcome.* It comes from a Greek word meaning energy or work. To pray effectually for someone is going to take energy. It is going to be work! And, as we read in this translation [ESV], it *has great power*!

When we pray, we should pray specifically with a desired outcome in mind. However, that outcome we have in mind is not always going to be what God has in His plan. Our desired outcome is not always going to be God's will. Isaiah 55:8 says *For My thoughts are not your thoughts, neither are your ways My ways, declares the Lord.* We don't always know God's will. His will is not always revealed to us. He reveals to us only the things that we need to know and at the time that we need to know them.

Psalm 18:30 says *This God—His way is perfect; the Word of the Lord proves true; He is a shield for all those who take refuge in Him.* We must realize that though we have in our minds a desired outcome, we should always pray that God's will be done. His desired outcome, in the grand scheme of things, is going to be so much better than ours! After all, *His way is perfect* [Psalm 18:30].

Fervent means *exhibiting or marked by great intensity of feeling*. How intense are my feelings for my friend? How deep is my knowledge of her burden? Is it a burden that I too bear or have born? Is my prayer for her *marked by great intensity of feeling*?

When we lift up a friend to Christ in prayer in order to bear her burden, are we acting effectually? Are we praying fervently? Ask yourself, is my prayer so specific to produce a desired outcome? Is it marked by great intensity? Or is it just *Lord, help Jane, she's having a hard time today*?

Our prayers should be effectual—*to produce a desired outcome*, and they must be fervent—*marked by great intensity*. Prayer is work!

When we say that our prayers need to be effectual to produce a desired outcome, we mean that they need to be specific, with specific results in mind. A good example of how our prayers need to be specific would be in the way we pray for our missionaries. I have, on occasion, heard someone pray, *Lord, bless all the missionaries around the world*. You may have heard this kind of prayer as well. Do we really want the Lord to bless *all* the missionaries? Certainly, we don't. There are missionaries around the world for every cult imaginable. Our intent in praying is not for the Lord to bless them all.

Be specific when you pray. When you pray for missionaries, call them by name and list their individual

Notes

Notes

needs. The same should be done when we lift up a friend to Christ. Be specific, call her by name, and list her specific needs. Pray effectually and pray fervently!

Another reason to pray specifically is so that we can see specific answers to our prayers. If I pray *bless so and so . . . how do I see that prayer answered?* It would be difficult. I like to see evidence of answered prayer. So, I get specific. I get detailed. I journal it! I write it down. I make a list. I tell God exactly who it is I am praying for [although He already knows], and I tell Him exactly what the need is in as much detail as I can. Then, when the answer comes, it's easily recognized as answered prayer.

Comforting Others

A passage that we will discuss in-depth later, but that is also quite appropriate now, is 2 Corinthians 1:3-4. The passage says *Blessed be the God and Father of our Lord Jesus Christ, the Father of mercies and God of all comfort, Who comforts us in all our affliction, so that we may be able to comfort those who are in any affliction, with the comfort with which we ourselves are comforted by God.*

Can you find in this passage the reason God comforts us? Read it again and see if it is not as clear and evident to you as it was to me.

Blessed be the God and Father of our Lord Jesus Christ. . . Who comforts us in all our affliction, so that we may be able to comfort those who are in any affliction, with the comfort with which we ourselves are comforted by God [2 Corinthians 1:3-4].

God comforts us so that we may comfort others! How will we comfort them? Or, with what will we comfort them? We comfort them *with the comfort with which we ourselves are comforted by God.* What a beautiful picture of God's love being manifested through us to others!

Can you imagine what a different world it would be, if we all loved others like God loves us, and we comforted others as He comforts us? What a beautiful picture of His great grace and undeniable mercy!

Do Not Grow Weary

How long do we bear a burden for another? Shortly after Paul tells us that we are to bear one another's burdens—the temporary overload—in Galatians 6:2, he writes in Galatians 6:9: *And let us not grow weary of doing good.* Weary, wow! It's so easy for us to grow weary, isn't it? In this fast-paced do-more, be-more world of drive-thru food and social media overload, we are almost born weary! But the Bible says *let us not grow weary.*

Weariness should never hinder us from wanting to see restoration in a friend who is in the midst of brokenness. Why should we not *grow weary of doing good*? The verse goes on to say *for in due season we will reap.* We will reap! That's our desire, isn't it? We want to reap. We want our prayers to be answered. We want that burden to be lifted. We want to be able to bear her burden, to give her relief. It says *we will reap* if we do these two things. First, if we do not *grow weary of doing good.* Second, if we do not give up. That's all. Don't grow weary

Notes

and don't give up! Don't get tired and don't quit! If we do these two things the Bible promises *we will reap*! We are to stay alongside the one in need until we see restoration. We cannot *grow weary of doing good* for in due season, *we will reap* if we don't quit. The Bible promises!

Until we see restoration—how long is that going to be? For some, it may be a very long time, maybe even years. But if we desire to reap, if we want to see results, we cannot *grow weary of doing good* and we cannot quit!

Loving as Christ Loves

If we read all of Galatians 6:2, we find that it not only says *bear one another's burdens*, but it also goes on to say *and so fulfill the law of Christ*. The first time I read this I wondered, as you may have, what law? What law of Christ will I fulfill by bearing another's burden? I did some research on this and here is what I found. The law that this passage speaks of, *the law of Christ*, is found back in John 13:34, where it says *A new commandment I give to you, that you love one another: just as I have loved you, you also are to love one another.* That is the law of Christ that Galatians 6:2 is talking about, *that you love one another: just as I have loved you. Bear ye one another's burdens and so fulfill the law of Christ—that ye love one another just as I have loved you.* That is what is going to happen when I bear the burden of another. I am going to develop a deep, deep love for that person, an even deeper love than I already have.

Do you know what is so wonderful about God's Word?

It not only tells us what to do, but how to do it. Not only do we read in John 13:34 about the law of Christ and that we are to love one another, but the verse also tells us how to love one another. Christ tells us in that verse that we are to love one another *just as I have loved you*. He is the greatest example of how to love that I know!

Just as I have loved you, He says. How has Christ loved us? Well, in Jeremiah 31:3 the Bible says *I have loved you with an everlasting love; therefore, I have continued My faithfulness to you.* He has loved me with an everlasting love! What an example—an everlasting love. A love that never gets weary of doing good. A love that does not give up. An everlasting, eternal kind of love!

We see that we are to love one another as Christ loves us. We see that He loves us with an everlasting love, and in 1 Corinthians 13:7, we see that *love bears all things*.

What does *bears all things* mean? It means to protect, to cover, to support. To do this, to be able to *bear all things*, including the burdens of others, we must be sensitive to their needs. In order to be sensitive to the needs of others we must first realize that we view the circumstances [the brokenness of life] through the lens of our own emotions. All of the things we have endured in our life should give us a greater compassion and love for those around us. The things we have been through tint the lens of our own emotions, and they help us bear one another up.

In the next chapter we will learn about the God of all comfort, and how we are the clay in the Potter's hands.

Notes

REFLECTION & APPLICATION

1. What did God teach me through this chapter?
2. How can I obediently respond to what I've learned?
3. What steps of faith does God want me to take now?

PRAYER & PETITIONS *Confession, Gratitude, Praise, and Requests*

MEDITATION & MEMORIZATION

Meditate on Galatians 6:1-10. Write out and memorize verse 9.

AND THE VESSEL HE WAS MAKING OF CLAY

WAS SPOILED IN THE POTTER'S HAND,

AND HE REWORKED IT INTO ANOTHER VESSEL,

AS IT SEEMED GOOD TO THE POTTER TO DO.

JEREMIAH 18:4

Chapter 6: THE GOD OF ALL COMFORT

And the vessel he was making of clay was spoiled in the potter's hand,

and he reworked it into another vessel,

as it seemed good to the potter to do. Jeremiah 18:4

SCRIPTURE TO MEDITATE ON
Psalm 147:3, Matthew 9:36, Hebrews 13:8 Write out one or more of these verses here.

In 2 Corinthians 1:3-4, we read *Blessed be the God and Father of our Lord Jesus Christ, the Father of mercies and God of all comfort, Who comforts us in all our affliction, so that we may be able to comfort those who are in any affliction, with the comfort with which we ourselves are comforted by God.*

We talked earlier in this book about these verses and the way we are to emulate God's love and compassion for us by passing that love and compassion on to others. He is *the Father of mercies.* He is the *God of all comfort.* He comforts us not just so we will be comforted, but that we in turn may with His comfort, love, endless compassion and mercy, comfort others.

The God of Peace

This, friend, is one of the best parts of the heart-healing process—when you get to take your brokenness and help someone else heal from theirs!

We have this assurance: In John 16:33 the Bible says *I have said these things to you, that in Me you may have peace.* Peace is available if we just ask for it. He's ready to give us His peace, if we will cast our burdens on Him.

But then He goes on in the same verse to say *in the world you will have tribulation*. There is no doubt about it. Tribulation will happen. Brokenness will happen, in your life and in mine.

After we read that peace is available and tribulation is inevitable, then here comes the wonderful assurance. He reminds us that even though we will have tribulation in the world, *I have overcome the world*. He has overcome the world! He is ready to give peace. He has overcome the tribulation this world deals out. Isn't it awesome to have the opportunity and privilege to serve the One Who is the giver of peace and the overcomer of this fallen world?

I wondered after I read verse 33, what were the things He said to them earlier? *I have said these things to you*. This is the last verse in chapter 16. So, I began reading in verse 1 of the chapter to find out what *these things* were.

In chapter 16 of John we find one of the last conversations Jesus had with His disciples before His arrest and crucifixion. It is basically a warning, a preparation in advance of oncoming tribulation, and the assurance of better things to come.

The chapter begins with, *I have said all these things to you,* and it ends with, *I have said all these things to you.* Interesting! The first verse says *I have said all these things to you to keep you from falling away.* The last verse says *I have said these things to you, that in Me you may have peace.* Between verses 1 and 33 Jesus tells His disciples 30 things that could make them fall away or separate them from the peace of God.

These 30 things are worth noting:

1. *They will put you out of the synagogues* [vs 2]
2. *Whosoever kills you will think he's doing God a service* [vs 2]
3. *I am going to Him that sent me* [vs 5]
4. *Sorrow has filled your heart* [vs 6]
5. *It is to your advantage that I go away* [vs 7]
6. *If I do not go away the Helper* [Holy Spirit] *will not come to you* [vs 7]
7. *When He* [the Helper] *comes He will convict the world concerning sin* [vs 8]
8. *I go to the Father* [vs 10]
9. *You will see me no longer* [vs 10]
10. *I still have many things to say to you but you cannot bear them now* [vs 12]
11. *When the Spirit of truth comes He will guide you into all truth* [vs 13]
12. *He* [the Spirit of truth] *will declare to you the things that are to come* [vs 13]
13. *A little while and you will see me no longer* [vs 16]
14. *You will weep and lament* [vs 20]

Notes

15. *The world will rejoice* [vs 20]

16. *You will be sorrowful* [vs 20]

17. *Your sorrow will turn into joy* [vs 20]

18. *You have sorrow now* [vs 22]

19. *But I will see you again* [vs 22]

20. *Your hearts will rejoice* [vs 22]

21. *No one will take your joy from you* [vs 22]

22. *Whatever you ask in My name He will give* [vs 23]

23. *Ask and you will receive that your joy be full* [vs 24]

24. *I have said these things in figures of speech* [vs 25]

25. *The hour is coming that I will tell you plainly* [vs 25]

26. *The Father Himself loves you* [vs 27]

27. *I came from the Father into the world* [vs 28]

28. *I will leave the world and go to the Father* [vs 28]

29. *You will be scattered each to his own home* [vs 32]

30. [You] *will leave Me alone yet I am not alone* [vs 32]

Jesus warned the disciples of all these things beforehand. He warned them to not be offended so that they will have peace. *In the world,* He says *you will have tribulation. But take heart; I have overcome the world.*

Jesus tells them that peace is available in Him. He is the only source of true peace. That's why it's called *the peace of God, which surpasses all understanding* [Philippians 4:7]. The world cannot understand this kind of peace, and it cannot give this kind of peace.

Sometimes we think that turning to God and relying on His mercy, grace and comfort will make our brokenness disappear. No, not necessarily. Relief from our brokenness may not always be the best thing for us. Relief is not always in His plan, but peace is.

We have to remember, we cannot see the big picture—but God can, and He is a God of mercy. He gives the strength, grace, and hope we need. He is always there to help us get through the brokenness in our lives.

Psalm 147:3 says *He heals the brokenhearted and binds up their wounds.* He is a Master at healing the broken hearted and binding up wounds. I know! Oh, isn't it great to have the Master healer and binder on our side?

Another assurance that He is the God of all comfort is found in Genesis 18:14 where the Lord asked Abraham, *Is anything too hard for the LORD*? I ask you today, Is there anything too hard for Him? NO! Even the impossible is not hard. Even the healing of a broken heart is not hard.

2 Corinthians 12:9 says *My grace is sufficient for you, for My power is made perfect in weakness.* His power is made perfect in my weakness! What a beautiful thought! I can cling to that thought. I can build my whole life around that thought. My heart can heal because of that thought.

The God of Compassion

We read in the Word of God that Jesus was moved with compassion. Just as He feels our burdens and is moved with compassion towards us, we are to feel the burdens of others and be moved with compassion towards them. Four times in the books of Matthew and Mark we find that Christ was moved with compassion.

When He saw the crowds, He had compassion for them,

Notes

because they were harassed and helpless, like sheep without a shepherd [Matthew 9:36].

When He went ashore, He saw a great crowd, and He had compassion on them and healed their sick [Matthew 14:14].

Moved with pity, He stretched out His hand and touched him and said to him, I will; be clean [Mark 1:41].

When He went ashore, He saw a great crowd, and He had compassion on them, because they were like sheep without a shepherd. And He began to teach them many things [Mark 6:34].

What is compassion? Webster's dictionary says it is the *sympathetic consciousness of others' distress* [or burdens] *together with a desire to alleviate it.* Sympathy, plus the desire to alleviate the burden or brokenness, equals compassion.

sympathy + desire to alleviate = compassion

You know, that's what Christ had for the people in the New Testament. He had compassion. He had compassion because they fainted, because they were scattered abroad, and because they had no shepherd.

And because of His compassion, He took action. His actions included healing the sick, putting forth His hand, touching them, speaking with them, cleansing them, and teaching them. These are the results of compassion.

He is not simply touched by the feeling of compassion; the Bible says He is *moved*. Moved to action by compassion. And His actions forever changed the lives of those He was moved with compassion toward!

Just like the people of the New Testament, Jesus is moved with compassion towards us as well. He is a God of compassion and He heals brokenness.

He binds brokenness up, He mends brokenness, and He knits brokenness back together, in His time.

The God of Second Chances

Have you ever thought of yourself as the *work of His hands* [Job 34:19]? We talked earlier about being the work of His hands when we looked at the emotional difference between each other as well as between us and our male counterparts. We are the work of His hands! Just like He made us special the first time, sometimes, He makes us over and special again.

Sometimes our lives become marred, blemished, flawed or stained. Or, maybe they're not exactly marred, but He knows that we can be so much more for His glory than we are right now. Just like in Jeremiah, we become that lump of clay on the potter's wheel. When we become that lump of clay in the hands of the Master Potter, the God of all comfort and compassion, the pain is never without purpose.

In Jeremiah 18:1-6, Jeremiah is told by the Lord to arise and go down to the potter's house and there he [Jeremiah] will hear the Words of the Lord. In verses 3-4, we find Jeremiah doing just as the Lord has said.

Notes

So, I went down to the potter's house, and there he was working at his wheel. And the vessel he was making of clay was spoiled in the potter's hand, and he reworked it into another vessel, as it seemed good to the potter to do [Jeremiah 18:3-4].

Then in verse 6, Jeremiah hears the Word of the Lord as He said *O house of Israel, can I not do with you as this potter has done? . . .Behold, like the clay in the potter's hand, so are you in My hand* [Jeremiah 18:6].

So, are we in God's hands? God used burdens in the lives of the Israelites to make them *as it seemed good to the potter to do*, and sometimes, He does the same in our lives.

We should never question God or anything He allows to enter our lives. Sometimes His tools are harsh, just as the potter saw it necessary to remake the vessel. But His mercy and grace are significantly greater! The pain is never without purpose, and it never lasts forever. This is a chapter in your life—this is not the whole book!

Romans 9:20 says *Will what is molded say to its molder, Why have you made me like this?*

Hebrews 13:8 says *Jesus Christ is the same yesterday, and today, and forever*. He was a God of compassion and God of all comfort to the Israelites, and the wonderful news is that He still is that same God to us today! He can be your God of compassion and your God of comfort if you will allow Him to be.

James 4:8 says *Draw near to God, and He will draw near*

to you. The God of all comfort is waiting for you to draw near to Him, so that He in turn, can draw near to you.

What are you waiting for? Draw near today!

We've looked at the solution: Casting our burdens, bearing up others, and the God of all comfort. Now let's move on to the final part of *The Heart That Heals*, Part Three, the application. This is where the rubber meets the road! How do we apply what we've learned?

In Part Three, we will discuss growing in Christ, what our response to burdens should be and the blessings of burdens. Then we'll wrap it all up with some very practical applications that I promise will be a help to you.

REFLECTION & APPLICATION

1. What did God teach me through this chapter?
2. How can I obediently respond to what I've learned?
3. What steps of faith does God want me to take now?

PRAYER & PETITIONS *Confession, Gratitude, Praise, and Requests*

MEDITATION & MEMORIZATION
Meditate on Jeremiah 18:1-4. Write out and memorize verse 4.

Part 3: THE APPLICATION

THUS YOU WILL

RECOGNIZE THEM

BY THEIR FRUITS.

MATTHEW 7:20

Chapter 7: GROWING IN CHRIST

Thus, you will recognize them by their fruits. Matthew 7:20

SCRIPTURE TO MEDITATE ON

1 Samuel 16:7b, Romans 3:10, 1 John 1:9 Write out one or more of these verses here.

What does it mean to grow in Christ, and how do we grow in Christ? Apart from how to know God's will, those are probably two of the most asked questions when it comes to living the Christian life.

Our Christian life should be a continual process of growing in Christ and becoming more like Him. This is what we call progressive sanctification. Sanctification is the process of being made or becoming holy. It literally means to be set apart for a unique purpose. That's exactly what begins to happen in our lives the moment we become a Christian. Sanctification is not an instantaneous thing; it's a process. The process is called growing in Christ.

More Like Him and Less Like Me

Genesis 1:26 tells us that we are made in His image. His desire for us is that we be like Him. Of course, we will never be fully like Him. However, we should always be striving to be more like Him and less like our old, sinful selves every day. More like Him. Less like me!

It sounds crazy for me to strive to be something I know I can never be. My desire though is not that I would be just like Him; I know I can't be that. Nevertheless, my desire is that I would be *more* like Him. More like Him today than I was yesterday, and less like my old sinful self today than I was yesterday—that is absolutely attainable! That's what we should strive for. Growing in Christ is a continual process of becoming more like Him and less like me, and that should be my desire.

Now that we know what it means, how do we do it? How do we grow in Christ?

We know that the obvious first step to growing in Christ is that we must know the Lord Jesus Christ as our personal Lord and Savior. We must be a born-again Christian in order to be able to grow in Christ.

Friend, if you are reading this book and you know that you are not a Christian, let's take care of that today. If you have never asked Him to come into your life, forgive you of your sins, and be your Lord and Savior, He wants to meet you where you are and be that for you today.

Or, maybe you think you might be a Christian, but you're just not 100% sure about your salvation and eternal security. Maybe you are not even sure what a Christian is or how to become one. It is for those reasons that I want to share with you today the simplicity of the Gospel of Jesus Christ, and how clear the plan of salvation is presented in the book of Romans.

What is a Christian? There are some specific characteristics that a Christian will exhibit, and while we know that *man looks on the outward appearance, but the Lord looks on the heart* [1 Samuel 16:7], it is by these characteristics that we distinguish the believer from the nonbeliever. Keep in mind though, that it is impossible for us to judge the heart of another. Only God truly knows the heart of man. Jeremiah 17: 9 says *The heart is deceitful above all things, and desperately sick; who can understand it?* Only God can truly know our hearts.

Characteristics of a Christian

Are you really born again? Does your life exhibit the following three characteristics? These characteristics will be made evident in the life of a true born-again believer—a Christian.

First, if you are a born-again Christian, you will have no habitual sin present in your life. The Bible says in 1 John 3:9 *No one born of God makes a practice of sinning, for God's seed abides in him; and he cannot keep on sinning, because he has been born of God.* This of course does not mean that we will never sin again after we have been born again. It simply means that because of our desire to please the Lord, we will not make a practice of habitual sin. We are not perfect, far from it.

Notes

2 Corinthians 5:17 says *Therefore, if anyone is in Christ, he is a new creation. The old has passed away; behold, the new has come.* If we sin, we should confess it to the Lord immediately. He has promised to forgive us. 1 John 1:9 says *If we confess our sins, He is faithful and just to forgive us our sins and to cleanse us from all unrighteousness.* As Christians we will not have habitual sin present in our lives.

Second, if you are a born-again Christian, you will have a desire to be more like Christ. 1 John 2:29 says *If you know that He is righteous, you may be sure that everyone who practices righteousness has been born of Him.* Christ is not only our Savior; He is our example. The Christian should always be striving to be more like Him. Jesus told His disciples in John 14:15 *If you love Me, you will keep my commandments.* As Christians we will have the desire to please the Lord Jesus in all that we do and say.

> *Just two choices on the shelf,*
> *pleasing God or pleasing self.* —Ken Collier

A Christian will not have the desire to follow after worldly things, but will have the desire to be more like Christ. As Christians, we have the desire to be more like Him and less like our old, sinful self, every single day.

Third, if you are a born-again Christian, you will have a love for others and a burden for the lost. 1 John 3:11 says *For this is the message that you have heard from the beginning, that we should love one another.* Romans 10:14 says *How then will they call on Him in Whom they have not believed? And how are they to believe in Him of*

Whom they have never heard? And how are they to hear *without someone preaching?* This should spur us to conviction and give us a desire to reach the world for Christ. As Christians we will have a love for others and a burden for the lost.

If you have any doubt whatsoever about your salvation, please take time to read carefully the following simple plan of salvation that is found in the book of Romans. Get this settled between you and God today so that you will know for sure where you will spend eternity.

Why Do I Need to Be Saved?

For all have sinned and fall short of the glory of God [Romans 3:23].

As it is written: None is righteous, no, not one [Romans 3:10].

Therefore, just as sin came into the world through one man [Adam], *and death through sin, and so death spread to all men because all sinned* [Romans 5:12].

What Does Sin Do to Me?

For the wages of sin is death, but the free gift of God is eternal life in Christ Jesus our Lord [Romans 6:23].

What Did Christ Do for Me?

But God shows His love for us in that while we were still sinners, Christ died for us [Romans 5:8].

Notes

Who Can Be Saved?

For everyone who calls on the name of the Lord will be saved [Romans 10:13].

What Do I Need to Do to Be Saved?

Because, you confess with your mouth that Jesus is Lord and believe in your heart that God raised Him from the dead, you will be saved. For with the heart one believes and is justified, and with the mouth one confesses and is saved [Romans 10:9-10].

If you are not sure about your salvation, please do not read another chapter of this book until you have taken care of the most important decision of your life. Here is a simple prayer that will guide you if you are ready to make that decision today.

Dear God,

I confess to You now that I am a sinner. I believe that You are the Son of God and that You died on the cross and shed your precious blood for my sins. I believe that You rose from the dead and are in Heaven today. I am placing my trust in You, Lord. Come into my heart, forgive me of my sins, and save me now. I commit myself to live for You,

Lord. Thank you for saving me.

In Jesus' name,

Amen

I hope if you prayed that prayer just now, you will let someone know. If you prayed and asked Jesus into your life, today is the day you begin to grow in Christ!

How to Grow in Christ

So, how do you grow in Christ? Here are four simple, yet vitally important, steps we as Christians need to take to assure that we are continually growing in Christ and becoming more like Him.

First, we need to be involved in a church that preaches and teaches the Word of God. Hebrews 10:25 says *Not neglecting to meet together, as is the habit of some, but encouraging one another, and all the more as you see the Day drawing near*. So much the more today, because we see the day [the coming of the Lord] approaching.

Time is short, and these times we live in are more evil than ever before. Trials and brokenness are more prevalent. It's important for the child of God to be in a church that preaches the Word of God. Where else are we going to get the encouragement we need? That kind of encouragement is only going to come from His Word and His people. It is so important that we be involved in a church that preaches and teaches the whole Word of God.

When I say involved, I don't mean just Sunday morning services. I mean involved! Attending Sunday School or small group regularly. Singing in the choir or playing in the orchestra, if that's your gift. Going to Bible study. Working in the children's ministry. Being a greeter.

Notes

Faithful on Sunday evenings and Wednesdays too. Whatever you can do to be a part of the fellowship of believers is going to help you grow in Christ. We should be involved in a church that preaches and teaches the whole Word of God in order to be continually growing in Christ and becoming more like Him.

Second, we need to be daily studying the Word of God. As it says in 2 Timothy 2:15 *Do your best to present yourself to God as one approved, a worker who has no need to be ashamed, rightly handling the Word of truth.* Studying God's Word, meditating on it, and memorizing Scripture should be a part of our daily routine.

We should build our lives on and around the Word of God. We must build His Word into our lives, as its core foundation, if we want to grow in Christ. His Word is the textbook for our lives. It's His love letter to us. It shows us how to live for Him and how to serve and please Him.

We wouldn't think of going a day without physical food, would we? Then why would we go a day without spiritual food? Isn't the spiritual food so much more important than the physical? We should be daily studying the Word of God in order to be continually growing in Christ and becoming more like Him.

Third, we need to be praying always and always be in an attitude of prayer. 1 Thessalonians 5:17-18 says *Pray without ceasing, give thanks in all circumstances; for this is the will of God in Christ Jesus for you*. We should always be in an attitude of prayer, giving thanks in every situation and for everything—not just the good things.

We need to give thanks for everything! We should be praying always and always be in an attitude of prayer in order to be continually growing in Christ and becoming more like Him.

Fourth, we need to be witnesses for Him and of all that He has done for us. Matthew 7:20 says *Thus you will recognize them by their fruits*. How many times have we seen God give strength to Christians and enable them, by His grace, to turn bad situations into good ones because of their testimony of His goodness?

There is no greater time for us to be a witness for Him than when we are enduring trials and brokenness. Those are the times when people are going to be watching us. They want to see if we practice what we preach. People want to know if our God is real. They want to see what we are really made of and if we can depend on Him for our every need. We need to be witnesses for Him and of all that He has done for us in order to be continually growing in Christ and becoming more like Him.

Continually Growing in Christ

We need to be continually growing in Christ and continually becoming more like Him. Genesis 1:26 says *Then God said, Let us make man in our image, after our likeness.* We were made in His image, for His glory, and for a unique purpose. His desire is for me to be like Him. He knows me, yet He still loves me. He wants me to be continually growing in Him and continually becoming more like Him. That must be my desire too.

Notes

I remember after my sister's death, the feeling I had of standing out in space on nothing, with nothing around me. I was in a lonely place, and I felt very alone! It was as if I were watching the world spin and spin and spin, watching life for everyone else go on when mine was at a complete and utter standstill. I couldn't seem to get back on that spinning world and back to life as I once knew it. Life there, in that world, continued for all the people around me, just as it had before. Most of them knew nothing of Ginger's death. But for me, life had come to a sudden, grinding, gut-wrenching, halt!

I just couldn't seem to get my life together. Things like picking up the dry cleaning, meeting appointments, paying bills, these things were no longer important to me. The brokenness inside me had taken over. The world and the people in it continued as before. But for me, I felt as if I was no longer a part of that world.

Maybe you feel much like that today. One thing I found was that I could not get my life back together—not by myself. I found that in order to get my life back together, I would need help. I would need God's help, and in a really, really big way! I knew I needed to continue to grow in Christ as I had grown in Him before I carried this burden. So, the question is, when we get to that point in our life, what should our response be? What should our response to burdens be? We'll look at that in the next chapter.

REFLECTION & APPLICATION

1. What did God teach me through this chapter?
2. How can I obediently respond to what I've learned?
3. What steps of faith does God want me to take now?

PRAYER & PETITIONS *Confession, Gratitude, Praise, and Requests*

MEDITATION & MEMORIZATION

Meditate on Matthew 7:15-20. Write out and memorize verse 20.

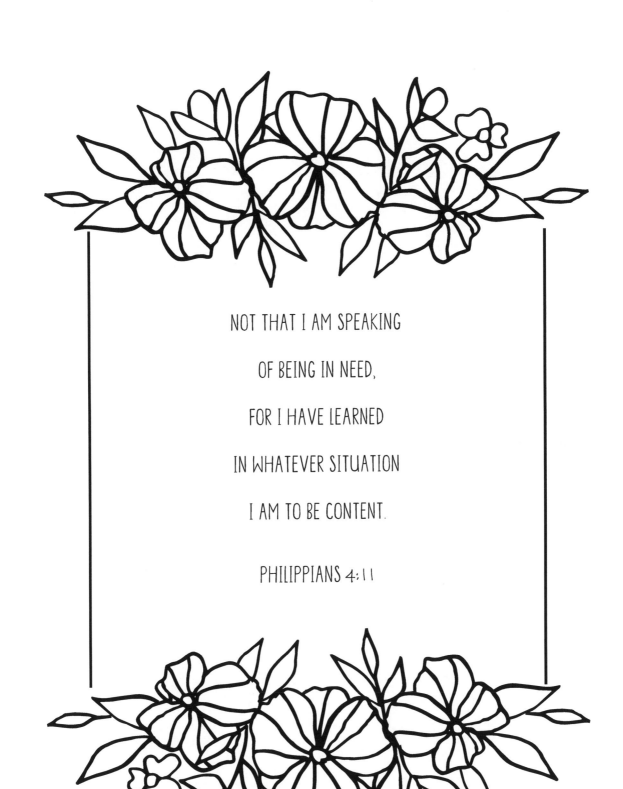

NOT THAT I AM SPEAKING

OF BEING IN NEED,

FOR I HAVE LEARNED

IN WHATEVER SITUATION

I AM TO BE CONTENT.

PHILIPPIANS 4:11

Chapter 8: OUR RESPONSE TO BURDENS

Not that I am speaking of being in need, for I have learned
in whatever situation I am to be content. Philippians 4:11

SCRIPTURE TO MEDITATE ON

Ephesians 4:31, Proverbs 4:23, Acts 16:25 Write out one or more of these verses here.

What should our response to burdens be—to our own burdens and to the burdens of others? I once read this little saying that has stuck in my mind for a very long time:

It's not situations that make us who we are, but
it's our response to situations that make us who we are.

It has served as a constant reminder of how much my response matters to God and to others, and how very important a correct response is.

We all respond to circumstances differently because we are all made differently. The situations we've been through are part of what makes us who we are.

Looking Through Different Lenses

Remember when we talked of bearing the burdens of others? We said that one of the things we must realize is that we view the circumstances, trials, test, brokenness of life through the lens of our own emotions. Well, that lens is developed in us as we ourselves go through the different circumstances, trials, tests, and brokenness.

That's one reason we all respond differently, because we are looking through different lenses. My lens is going to be tinted just a little bit different than yours. It may be a bit weaker, or it may be a bit stronger. It may be lighter, or it may be darker.

I read an illustration of a tea bag and found the analogy quite interesting. Have you ever thought of how a tea bag responds to the hot water it is steeped in? There is a lesson to be learned from the tea bag!

When we take a tea bag, place it in a teacup, and fill the cup with hot water, the water activates the tea in the bag unleashing its taste into the water around it. The hot water didn't create the taste; it merely revealed, or drew out, what was already in the bag.

This depicts what happens in the human heart. The pressures around us merely draw out of our heart what is already in it. We cannot blame the hot water for the taste in the cup. The contents of the tea bag determine the flavor of the tea. What flavor is your tea?

J. Allan Petersen. *Your Reactions Are Showing.* Lincoln, NE: Back to the Bible; 1967. p. 3

Our response not only makes us who we are, but it also comes from who we are.

I remember very clearly and vividly, my thoughts after I learned of my sister's death. I thought, *Lord, I had no idea that you intended for Ginger to only live eighteen years.* My response could have been anger or bitterness. But instead, the lens of my response was tinted by my belief that God was in control. I believed that He was in control even though my understanding of His plan was limited.

However, I did not develop that response overnight. It was a response developed over a lifetime as I learned to lean on the Lord for every need and realized that He is always in total control of every situation.

Nothing slips by God. Nothing catches Him off guard or takes Him by surprise, as it does us. He is always in control, always prepared and always waiting and able to meet your particular need, whatever that may be.

God leads us along the pathway of life one step at a time. Sometimes He takes us up steep, treacherous hills, too big for us to climb. Sometimes through deep water where we feel we're going to drown. Sometimes through the parched, barren desert. Don't let anyone ever tell you He won't give you more than you can handle. He will! This is how and when we develop our dependence on Him. His *grace is sufficient* [2 Corinthians 12:9]. If we were never led up steep treacherous hills, through deep waters and barren deserts, how would we ever learn to depend on His all-sufficient grace?

Notes

Learning to Be Content

Sometimes, our response to burdens may just need to be contentment. Paul says in Philippians 4:11 *for I have learned in whatever situation I am to be content*. How do you think Paul learned to be content? Notice that the verse doesn't say he was content, it says that he learned to be content. We can assume that at some point Paul was not content. He had to learn to be content.

He certainly had plenty of opportunities in his life not to be content, and plenty of opportunities to learn contentment. Paul learned so well to be content that he and his friend Silas sang songs while imprisoned. Acts 16:25 says *About midnight Paul and Silas were praying and singing hymns to God, and the prisoners were listening to them.* And the prisoners were listening to them!

If we read the complete passage, we find that Paul and Silas had been followed for days by a young woman possessed with an evil spirit. The men that controlled her made money by using her. No doubt this was the human trafficking of that day. When Paul commanded the evil spirit to come out of her, it did, and their money-making opportunity ceased to be.

The men caught up with Paul and Silas. They brought them into the marketplace and to the magistrates. Paul and Silas were accused of being Jews, causing trouble, and teaching things that were unlawful. The Bible says a multitude rose up together against them, their clothes were torn off, and they were beaten. Then they were cast into prison, but not just the regular prison. They were cast into the innermost secure part of the prison. There their feet were put in stocks, and yet they sang. And yet they sang! And the prisoners were listening to them!

There in the inner part of that prison, with his feet in stocks, Paul was content. Just as Paul learned to be content, we too must sometimes learn just to be content. Contentment in this situation afforded Paul the opportunity to be a testimony of God's goodness and faithfulness. And because of Paul's contentment, the jailor and his entire household were saved! Precious souls, saved from an eternity in hell, because of contentment! It wasn't just the prisoners listening.

Do you think your response matters? It does! Do you think contentment matters? It does! Sometimes, God just wants to see if we can be content and rest in Him. *Whatever situation I am in, I am to be content.*

The Works of God Are on Display

Another reason we need to be sure that our response is right is found in John 9:2-3. In this passage we find Jesus passing by a blind man, and the disciples asked Jesus, *who sinned, this man or his parents, that he was born blind*? Jesus answers them, *It was not that this man sinned, or his parents, but that the works of God might be displayed in him*. Our response to trials, to brokenness, to burdens must be right so *that the works of God might be displayed in* our lives.

What happens if our response is not right and *the works of God* cannot *be displayed in* us? What would have

Notes

Notes

happened if Job had cursed God? What if Lot had looked back at Sodom and Gomorrah? What if Paul, the greatest missionary ever, had given up after his first imprisonment? What if Joseph had had his brothers thrown in jail for what they did to him? All of these people had the right response, and God was *displayed* in their lives.

You certainly can imagine though, in each of these situations, how history could have been altered. Lives could have been changed, and not for the better. There is even the possibility that civilizations could have been altered, forever, had these faithful servants of God not had the correct response to burdens.

What about your response? What about my response? Have we allowed God to be *displayed* in our lives through the presence of trials and brokenness? Is it evident that we are trusting in Him? Our response to burdens matters.

What If We Don't Know How to Respond?

Sometimes, when attempting to bear the burden of another, we simply don't know how to respond. This is especially true if we haven't been down that road before, if we haven't experienced that particular kind of brokenness.

Remember what Solomon says in Ecclesiastes 3:7. He says that there is *a time to keep silence, and a time to speak.* Possibly, we don't need to speak at all. Maybe it is just *a time to keep silence*. The burdened friend may just need us to sit with them in silence. Sometimes that is the greatest comfort we can give, and that is the response that is needed at that particular time.

Other ways we can respond to a friend with a burden is to make contact with them often. Invite them to share and participate in activities, or sit with them in church. A touch or a hug can mean so much. Identify with them as much as possible. Pray for them often, pray specifically, and pray with them as well.

Our Response Affects Others

Not only does our response to burdens make us who we are, but as mothers, how we respond to our burdens and to the burdens of others can also make our children who they are.

I heard a very wise man say one time that *your children are a message sent to a place you'll never go*, and you know, that is so very true! Our children are like little messengers that we send out to a lifetime of places that we will never go, and a lifetime of people we will never know. They are also like little sponges. They soak up everything! Your response to burdens matters.

There is no greater blessing, no greater joy as a parent, than to have raised an excellent messenger! 3 John 1:4 says *I have no greater joy than to hear that my children are walking in the truth.* What a wonderful thing it is to have your children be that message of truth to the next generation.

After my sister's funeral, we rode in the police escorted

Notes

procession. We were traveling in the car directly behind the escort vehicle. My father was driving, my mother beside him, and my husband and I were in the back seat. The procession left the church and headed north up U.S. Route 19. If you are in any way familiar with this highway in Florida, you know it runs along the Gulf Coast. It's a long, straight, flat, four-lane, divided highway. On a clear day you can see for miles down that road. After several minutes of driving, my husband tapped me on the shoulder and said, *Turn around and look*. To my astonishment, when I turned and looked out the back window, I could not believe what my eyes were seeing! As far as my eyes could physically see, there was following us a double line of cars with their lights on. Tears still come when I think of this precious memory! And I don't cry much.

My sister had become that message! She had become a message sent to a place my parents would never go. She had become a message sent to a people they would never know.

I knew the church was packed that day, but I had no idea until someone told me weeks later that it was standing room only. I did not know that the lobby was filled with people and that people were even standing outside.

My sister was a message. Our children are a message, and that is why it is so important that our response to burdens be the correct response. Sponges are waiting to soak up our response!

Not only does our response matter when it comes to our

children, but as wives, our response to burdens and brokenness can certainly affect our husbands. As grandmothers, our response can affect our grandchildren. As single women and women in the church, our response can make or break our testimony. This is especially true in a time of great crisis, and even more so if you are in any type of leadership position in your church. People want to see what you are truly made of. They want to know if you practice what you preach. They want to see if your faith is real, if your life is real— and they'll find out too!

No matter your age, no matter how young or old you are, there is always someone watching you. This was made very apparent to my oldest daughter, who in her senior year of high school worked as a teacher's aide in a K4 classroom. One Sunday afternoon after church, our family went out for dinner. After we were seated, a family I did not recognize with a four-year-old girl entered the restaurant. Right away this little girl spotted my daughter from across the crowded room. She began to tug at her daddy's coat and announce loudly with her arm outstretched and finger pointed in my daughter's direction, *Daddy, that's Rachel, Daddy, that's Rachel*! My daughter realized that day how important her words, actions, and deeds were, because a little four-year-old girl was watching. Our response really does make a difference. It matters for a lot of reasons and to a lot of people. But let's keep in mind, that most importantly, our response matters to God.

Notes

Notes

Roots of Bitterness

The Bible warns against it, and it is important for us to guard against it. What is *it*? It is a root of bitterness. Hebrews 12:15 says *See to it that no one fails* [lest our testimony be a stumbling block to others] *to obtain the grace of God; that no root of bitterness springs up and causes trouble, and by it many become defiled.*

Bitterness in our lives will only accomplish three things.

1. It will make us a stumbling block to others
2. It will cause us trouble
3. It will cause many to be defiled

None of us want to be a stumbling block. None of us want to be troubled. And I am sure none of us want to be responsible for the defilement of others.

To God, bitterness is a very serious offense, and it should be to us as well. Look at the magnitude of the seriousness of this *root of bitterness*. Look what it is listed with here in this passage. Verse 16 goes on to say *that no one is sexually immoral or unholy like Esau, who sold his birthright for a single meal.* Bitterness is a serious mistake!

Bitterness will not only affect our testimony, which in turn affects others, but it will also affect us. Verse 15 says *that no root of bitterness springs up and causes trouble.* God does not want bitterness to trouble us. However, bitterness will trouble us, if we allow it to.

Job says that bitterness is worse than death. In Job 9:18 he says *He will not let me get my breath* [my life], *but fills me with bitterness.* It would be better if I were dead, Job says, but instead, I am filled with bitterness.

Bitterness will affect you physically. Proverbs 4:23 says *Keep your heart with all vigilance, for from it flow the springs of life.* I could have easily become bitter after my sister's death. I could have allowed a root of bitterness to spring up for many reasons other than just the fact that she was taken from us at such a young age. I could have been bitter because she was my only sibling. Now all of a sudden, I am an only child. I could have been bitter because she was the one who had elected to care for my parents when they were old—she really got out of that one! Now I am the one who will care for them. [She would have done a much better job!] I could have been bitter when we went to court against the man who killed her in a county that was said to be the toughest in Florida on DUI cases. He got off with just probation.

It certainly would have been easy for me to become bitter the day that decision was handed down. Instead, I chose to praise God! I praised God that day that my sister was the one that was killed, and not the one that killed. I would rather her be dead than to have to live the rest of her life facing the fact that she had killed someone.

Bitterness will trouble you, friend. It will eat you up inside if you allow it to. It will trouble your heart if you are not careful, *for from it* [the heart] *flow the springs of life.*

Do you remember in Ruth 1:19 when Naomi, who was filled with bitterness, returned to her home in Bethlehem with her daughter-in-law, Ruth? It had only been ten

Notes

years since Naomi left Bethlehem. During that time, she had lost her husband and two sons. The bitterness that she was now filled with had so affected her countenance that the people of Bethlehem, her friends, did not even recognize her! They asked, *Is this Naomi*? She was so filled with bitterness that she says in verse 20, *Do not call me Naomi; call me Mara*, which means bitter.

Ephesians 4:31 warns us to *Let all bitterness and wrath and anger and clamor and slander be put away from you, along with all malice.* If we look back up to verse 30 in that same passage, we see why; it grieves the Holy Spirit.

In Job 1:13-19, we read how that in the span of one day's time, Job, a man the Bible calls *blameless and upright, and one that feared God, and turned away from evil*, a man who was *the greatest of all the people of the east*, lost almost everything he had. All in just one day! Job lost on that one day five hundred oxen, five hundred donkeys, seven thousand sheep, and three thousand camels. If that alone were not enough, he also lost seven sons and three daughters—ten children in all, and an untold number of servants. What would you or I do under these extreme circumstances?

Look what the Bible records that Job, *the greatest of all the people of the east*, did. Job 1:20-22 says *Then Job arose and tore his robe and shaved his head and fell on the ground and worshiped. And he said, Naked I came from my mother's womb, and naked shall I return. The Lord gave, and the Lord has taken away; blessed be the name of the Lord.* Verse 22 should be an example and inspiration to us all, it says *In all this Job did not sin or charge God with wrong.*

How can we question God's working in our lives, and how can we allow a root of bitterness to spring up troubling us and grieving the Holy Spirit? Our response to burdens must be a right response. I have found in my own life that when I can view my burdens and brokenness as a blessing, right responses come much more naturally. Can burdens really be a blessing? Yes, they can! And we'll find out how in the next chapter.

REFLECTION & APPLICATION

1. What did God teach me through this chapter?
2. How can I obediently respond to what I've learned?
3. What steps of faith does God want me to take now?

PRAYER & PETITIONS *Confession, Gratitude, Praise, and Requests*

MEDITATION & MEMORIZATION
Meditate on Philippians 4:10-20. Write out and memorize verse 11.

THE LORD UPHOLDS

ALL WHO ARE FALLING AND

RAISES UP ALL

WHO ARE BOWED DOWN.

PSALM 145:14

Chapter 9: THE BLESSINGS OF BURDENS

The Lord upholds all who are falling and raises

up all who are bowed down. Psalm 145:14

SCRIPTURE TO MEDITATE ON
Exodus 1:12a, Genesis 50:19-20, Acts 5:42 Write out one or more of these verses here.

I have often thought that if there are any blessings in having burdens, and there are, one of them must be that burdens give us a greater sensitivity and compassion to recognize burdens in others. I have certainly found that to be true in my own life. You may have found this to be true in yours as well.

The Israelites were made better because of the burdens put on them by the Egyptians. It says in Exodus 1:12a *But the more they* [the Israelites] *were oppressed, the more they multiplied.* The Egyptians tried to wear them down. They mistreated them and forced them into slavery. But instead of giving up, the Israelites just grew stronger and multiplied. They thrived!

When we are burdened or mistreated, we may feel defeated. However, our burdens can actually make us stronger. They can also develop character qualities in us that prepare us for what God has planned for our future.

Notes

Rejoice in Suffering

But there is yet another blessing of burdens that is found in Romans 5. Verses 1-2 say *Therefore, since we have been justified by faith, we have peace with God through our Lord Jesus Christ. Through Him we have also obtained access by faith into this grace in which we stand, and we rejoice in hope of the glory of God.*

Look at all of these wonderful privileges listed here that we as Christians have:

1. We are justified by faith
2. We have peace with God
3. We have access by faith
4. We stand in grace
5. We rejoice in hope

Paul goes on to say in verses 3-5, *More than that*, not only all of this that is listed above, not only do we have all of these privileges as children of God, but *we rejoice in our sufferings* also. Not only are we justified by faith; not only do we have peace with God and access by faith; not only do we stand in grace and rejoice in hope; not only all of this, but we also rejoice in our sufferings!

Why? Why would anyone in their right mind rejoice in suffering? Why did Paul rejoice in his suffering? The passage goes on to say that Paul rejoiced in his suffering because *knowing that suffering produces endurance, and endurance produces character, and character produces hope*. The end result of suffering is hope. Suffering produces endurance. Endurance produces character, and character produces the end result, which is hope.

suffering —> endurance —> character —> hope

Notes

But that's not all. Hold on! It gets even better. Paul goes on to explain in verse 5 *and hope* [the end result of suffering] *does not put us to shame*. Why? Why does hope not put us to shame? Hope does not put us to shame *because God's love has been poured into our hearts through the Holy Spirit Who has been given to us*.

Remember that the end result of suffering is hope? Now we see that the result of hope is *God's love has been poured into our hearts*. The love of God *poured into our hearts* is the result of hope. I love the use of the word *poured* here. His love isn't just sprinkled on our hearts. It isn't just a splattering of His love. It is a deluge! A deluge of love *poured into our hearts*!

The end result of suffering is hope, and the end result of hope is a deluge of God's love *poured into our hearts*! Our hearts are flooded with His love.

A Common Bond

Suffering, trials, burdens, brokenness—they all bring us together; they give us a closeness as nothing else can do. They give us who have experienced them a common bond, and the result is the love of God being shed abroad in our hearts.

We were all witnesses to the common bond that developed among the people of New York City on and after September 11, 2001. You may have experienced a similar bond with your own family or circle of friends

- 109 -

Notes

after a tragedy developed in your life or theirs.

My family developed such a bond on December 12, 1987. We look at things differently now. The phone ringing late at night sends a chill through us. The words *I love you* and hugs mean more now. We enjoy life and being with each other more because we know that today could be the last for any of us. Goodbyes are tougher. Laughter is sweeter. Cards and notes are more meaningful, and birthdays are more celebrated.

A common bond is a special thing, whether it is born of tragedy or happy times. We all need this kind of bond with others. It too is one of the blessings of burdens.

Remember the quote by C.S. Lewis on one of the first pages of this journal— the *HOW TO GET THE MOST OUT OF THIS BOOK* page?

Friendship is born at that moment when one person says to another: What! You too? I thought I was the only one.

You are not the only one. I am not the only one, and that is why I'm sharing my journey with you today. We're in this boat together, and God is at the helm!

Being Held

Another blessing of burdens is the blessing of a God Who upholds us. It says in Psalm 145:14 *The Lord upholds all who are falling and raises up all who are bowed down.* Sometimes our burden, our brokenness, seems to be far more than we could ever bear. Maybe you're there. You may wonder, *how can I go on bearing this burden*?

All we can do is give those burdens to the Lord. I call Him my *Great Burden-Bearer*. Chapter 145 of Psalms holds a multitude of evidence as to how and why God is able to uphold the fallen. Just look at these wonderful promises!

- His greatness is unsearchable [vs 3]
- He does mighty acts across generations [vs 4]
- He is full of glorious splendor and majesty [vs 5]
- He does wondrous works [vs 5-6]
- He is righteous [vs 7]
- He is gracious and merciful and abounding in steadfast love [vs 8]
- He is good to all and [again] merciful [vs 9]
- His kingdom is an everlasting kingdom [vs 13]
- He is the source of all of our daily needs [vs 15-16]
- He is righteous in all His ways and kind [vs 17]
- He is near to all who call on Him in truth [vs 18]
- He hears our cries and saves us [vs 19]
- He preserves us [vs 20]

These verses should be an encouragement to anyone who is fallen, burdened, or broken. He is just waiting to lift us up. He wants to uphold us!

In Matthew 11:28-29 Jesus says *Come to Me, all who labor and are heavy laden* [all those that are burdened, all those who are broken], *and I will give you rest. Take My yoke upon you, and learn from Me* [*Be still, and know that I am God*], *for I am gentle and lowly in heart, and you will find rest for your souls.* You will find rest for your soul!

Come to Him and *find rest for your soul*. What a comfort and blessing to have a God like that!

Notes

Suffering for Christ

Maybe you are suffering today for the cause of Christ. Maybe your burden is one of tribulation because of your faith in Christ, because you have chosen to be a Christian. The way our culture is headed, that is becoming more and more common.

In Acts 5:41 Luke says *Then they left the presence of the council, rejoicing that they were counted worthy to suffer dishonor for the name.* Have you ever thought of persecution as being a blessing? It can be. It certainly would push us to be more Christlike. But are we *worthy to suffer dishonor for the name*?

I have a friend who frequently travels to China to minister to the underground churches and their pastors. I remember the story he told of a pastor whose son was jailed because of his faith in Jesus Christ. The friend tells how the pastor felt honored that his son was found *worthy to suffer dishonor for the name* of Christ. When the pastor was asked if we should pray for the religious persecution in China to stop, he said, *No! The persecution makes the church stronger.* This, too, is the blessing of a burden— the church grows stronger. We grow stronger.

In Acts chapter 5, Luke recounts the events of Peter and John being persecuted. They were physically abused for their faith in Jesus Christ. Both of these disciples knew how Jesus had suffered, and they counted it a privilege to suffer for His sake. It was a privilege for them to be found *worthy to suffer dishonor for the name.*

In Matthew 5:11-12 we read: *Blessed are you when*

others revile you and persecute you and utter all kinds of evil against you falsely on My account. Rejoice and be glad, for your reward is great in heaven, for so they persecuted the prophets who were before you. The blessing of a burden, the blessing of persecution— *for your reward is great in heaven.*

If this is the boat you are in today, friend, you're in good company, you're in a good boat, *for so they persecuted the prophets who were before you.*

We find in Acts 5:42 that the burden of persecution was a blessing, as it formed the first home Bible study. In Acts 8:1-4, Acts 11:20-21, and 1 Peter 1:1, we also see that the burden of persecution was a blessing, as it was a springboard for the spread of the gospel.

In Galatians 5:11, we see that the burden of persecution is the proving ground that Paul was preaching the truth. What is our *proving ground*? Are we teaching and spreading the truth? Is our lifestyle a picture of truth? Is there proof? The burden of persecution could be that proof. Burdens certainly can be a blessing.

Trusting Him More

Another blessing of having a burden is that it gives us greater opportunities for trusting God. Job lost almost everything he had: his family, his wealth, and even his health. Through all of this, God never revealed to Job the purpose for his burdens. He never revealed to Job that Satan himself had challenged Job's motives for serving God. Job's friends, even his wife, turned against him after

he lost everything. But Job just kept on trusting God!

Do we trust in the Almighty God through our burdens? What about when everyone else turns against us? Can we still trust Him?

God Meant it for Good

Another blessing of burdens—God meant it for good. *A young man in his teens, living in a Middle Eastern country, was kidnapped and sold to slave traders. Carried across the border into a foreign nation, he was there framed and falsely accused of a serious crime. He languished in prison for several years until, through an incredible turn of events, he was catapulted to a position of enormous power and influence within the government of that foreign country—a position he then used to rescue his own kidnappers.* —Layton Talbert. *Not by Chance.* Greenville, SC: Bob Jones University Press; 2001. p. 1

In Genesis 50:19-20, Joseph finally, after years of bearing the burden of being kidnapped, sold to slave traders, falsely accused, thrown in prison, and forgotten, faces his kidnappers—his own brothers. This is what he has to say to them: *Do not fear, for am I in the place of God? As for you, you meant evil against me, but God meant it for good, to bring it about that many people should be kept alive, as they are today.*

God meant it for good! We cannot always see this blessing right away. There could be times that we may never know how *God meant it for good*. It is a blessing, however, to know that everything, even the burdens and brokenness that come into our lives, are a result of a God we can trust! To know that in His infinite plan, He meant it for our good, is a blessing of the burden.

In this last section of *The Heart That Heals*, we've looked at growing in Christ, what our response to burdens should be, and the blessings of burdens. In the final chapter we will wrap it all up with some practical applications.

REFLECTION & APPLICATION

1. What did God teach me through this chapter?
2. How can I obediently respond to what I've learned?
3. What steps of faith does God want me to take now?

PRAYER & PETITIONS *Confession, Gratitude, Praise, and Requests*

MEDITATION & MEMORIZATION
Meditate on Psalm 145. Write out and memorize verse 14.

BLESSED IS THE MAN [WOMAN] WHO… DELIGHT [S] IN

THE LAW OF THE LORD, AND… MEDITATES DAY AND NIGHT.

[S]HE IS LIKE A TREE PLANTED BY STREAMS OF WATER.

PSALM 1:1-3

Chapter 10: PRACTICAL APPLICATIONS

Blessed is the man [woman] who . . . delight[s] in

the law of the Lord, and . . . meditates day and night.

[S]he is like a tree planted by streams of water. Psalm 1:1-3

SCRIPTURE TO MEDITATE ON
Psalm 18:30, Isaiah 55:8, Psalm 46:10 Write out one or more of these verses here.

Throughout my journey, to learn to *Be still, and know that I am God*, God has also shown me other things that have helped my heart to heal from its brokenness. This chapter is full of practical applications. It may just be that I've saved the best for last!

Listed in this chapter you will find ten practical applications that God has shown me that have helped me personally to heal my brokenness. I hope that they will be a help to you as well, and I hope you will share them with your broken friends.

1 **Burdens give us opportunities that we otherwise may not have had.** They give us the opportunity to draw closer to God and to each other. Through burdens and brokenness, we learn to depend on God. We grow closer to Him, and we develop a common bond with others.

Several years ago, my mother had breast cancer. No doubt you know someone who has cancer, had cancer, or maybe that someone is even you. My mother will tell you today that she would not choose to not have had that burden placed on her if she could. The burden of cancer gave her opportunities to testify of God's goodness that she otherwise would not have had. She drew closer to Him and developed a new dependence on Him as well.

My mother also developed a common bond with millions of other women. Most of them she will never meet, but to those she has met, she has been a tremendous encouragement! For friends just hearing the diagnosis, she has been able to be a comfort and a stream of information.

When you endure through the fiery trials of a burden, when your brokenness is healed, look for those God wants you to bear up. Ask Him to show you the person, in their brokenness. I am a firm believer that God puts us through trials much of the time just so we can bear up others, and with His compassion, we can be Jesus' hands to them. Burdens give us opportunities we may not have had otherwise.

2 **Burdens strengthen our prayer life in ways that nothing else can do.** I remember many years ago when a friend of mine, the athletic director at the school my children attended, dislocated his shoulder. If you have ever experienced a dislocated shoulder, you know how debilitating and painful it can be. I broke my collar bone once. I don't know if this would compare, but it was for sure debilitating! My friend was unable to work. He couldn't even teach class for several days. I recall his precious testimony of how God used that time in his life to draw him closer. His prayer life was strengthened because of the time he spent alone with God. Sometimes God uses burdens in our lives just to draw us closer to Him, and that is a beautiful thing—that is a blessing!

3 **Burdens make us more compassionate.** Not only do burdens give us compassion that we may not otherwise have had, they also help us empathize in a way we could not before the burden. There is a difference between sympathy and empathy. Sympathy is my ability to feel compassion, sorrow, or pity for someone with a burden. Empathy, on the other hand, is me putting myself in the shoes of that person.

When I have been through a burden myself, it gives me the unique ability to feel empathy, and not just sympathy. Empathy is a stronger emotion and creates a stronger bond. Burdens make us more compassionate and they give us the ability to empathize.

4 Burdens strengthen our testimony before others. Burdens not only give us the opportunity to edify and lift each other up, but they also give us opportunities to be a testimony of God's goodness. Remember when I told you about looking back at the funeral procession after my sister's funeral? All of those hundreds of people were opportunities for us to be a testimony of God's goodness. There are people around you, watching, especially during times of trials and tribulation. They are watching you in your brokenness. They want to see if your faith is real. There is no better time to be a testimony of His goodness. Look for the opportunities!

5 Start an encouragement file. One of the biggest files I have in my office today is my encouragement file. Years ago, at the suggestion of a mentor I started that file, and I am so glad I did! That file is precious to me today. If there were a fire and I had only moments to grab files and escape, that file would be one of the ones I would grab. There are letters, notes, and cards of encouragement from a four-year-old to a ninety-year-old in that file. Whenever I am feeling sad, I can go to that file and pull something out that will be an encouragement to me. Many of the items in that file provide me with spiritual encouragement as well. My encouragement file is just all that — encouragement for this weary soul. Start an encouragement file today!

6 With that being said, add to someone else's encouragement file! Write a thank you note to someone who has impacted your life. It is difficult for a thankful person to become a bitter person or to be discouraged. When we are thankful, we are less likely to look at what we see as the bad in our lives and more likely to see the good.

One of the first things I did to help my heart heal after my sister's death [and it was actually several months after her death when I began this] and again, at the counsel of a mentor, was to begin writing thank you notes. I wrote to everyone God brought to my mind that had had an impact on my life—especially if that impact was of a spiritual nature. I first started as far back as I could remember, probably when I was four or five years old. It is one of the best pieces of advice I can give you, and one of the best things I did to heal my brokenness.

You will find that when you enter into an attitude of gratefulness for all that has been done for you, you will likely see how wonderfully you have been blessed! You will see how the Lord has brought certain people and certain circumstances across the pathway of your life to mold you and to make you all that you are today. Add to someone's encouragement file today. Write a note of thanks. You'll be glad you did!

7 **Beware of the effects of color, music, the foods you eat, and even what you wear.** I'm not going to go into a great deal of detail here, but let me just expand on the effect color can have in your life.

I am an artist and kind of into marketing. I have studied the effects colors have on us and the different feelings they invoke. The advertising world and marketing professionals have known this stuff for years, and they use it extensively to their advantage.

I remember when my younger son was about eight years old, and our family dentist suggested that we take him to a pediatric dentist because of some special problems he had with his teeth. The pediatric dentist he sent us to had an office in the same building but directly across the hall from the orthodontist we used. I enjoyed going to the orthodontist's office because it was painted floor-to-ceiling like Key West, Florida. [Apparently the orthodontist had an obsession with Key West, and no doubt we helped fund his adventures.] The colors in that office were light, bright, and uplifting. The entire office was a virtual work of art. I loved going there!

The pediatric dentist office across the hall, however, was a different story! It wasn't until about our third or fourth visit to that office that I began to realize the psychological effect that color can play on a person. I had read about it but never experienced it for myself in such a profound and unexpected way.

The pediatric dentist office was much like the orthodontist office, a work of art from floor to ceiling, and maybe even more so because of the amount of detailed work that was displayed there. But the dentist office was painted floor-to-ceiling like a jungle—not like Key West. The colors were dark and depressing, not light and calming like the orthodontist office.

My son and I visited that office at least once every six months for several years, and every time I left, I would feel an overwhelming sense of oppression and anxiety. I finally asked our family dentist to take my son back into his practice—all because of the colors on the walls of the pediatric dentist office and the oppressive feelings it left me with.

The effects that colors can have on us is well documented. The color black gives the impression of authority and power; it is stylish and timeless. The color white implies innocence, purity, and sterility. Red is an emotionally intense color; it stimulates a faster heartbeat and breathing. Pink is a tranquilizing color. I've even read of sports teams that paint the opposing team's locker rooms pink, so that their opponents will lose energy! Blue, too, is a tranquil and peaceful color—like the blues of Key West. It is one of the most popular colors. Studies show that people are more productive in blue rooms. It has been reported that the color blue actually causes our bodies to produce calming chemicals. No wonder God made the sky and ocean blue. No wonder we find the waters of the Caribbean so calming and relaxing. The orthodontist office was mostly blue. Green is a calming, refreshing color. Television stations often have guests who are waiting to appear sit in greenrooms to relax. Yellow is a cheerful color; it is considered to be an optimistic color and is said to enhance concentration. That's why legal pads are yellow. Brown implies something that is solid, reliable, and genuine. When I first read about brown, I thought about that package delivery company that drives the big brown trucks—they'd like that.

Colors certainly can have a big role in the way you and I feel, and we may not even realize it. Just as colors can affect us, so can the music we listen to, the foods we choose to eat, and the clothes we wear.

I remember when a friend of mine explained to me the routine he followed before taking college exams. One of the last things he always did was to put on his favorite outfit, the one he felt best in. It would always be something very nice, dressy, and something he felt comfortable wearing. He had read studies of how students tested better when wearing their best clothes.

In a similar way, I found this to be true in my own life. When I come home from a long day's work, I have two choices. I can either keep my work clothes on or I can change into something more comfortable. If I change into something more comfortable, it's usually sweat pants and a t-shirt. I have found though that I accomplish much more and feel more energetic if I just keep my work clothes on. If I change and put on that worn-out, comfortable pair of sweat pants and ragged old t-shirt, my energy level drops dramatically, and consequently I am much less productive. So, all that being said, beware of the effects of color, music, the foods you eat, and even what you wear.

8 Look for the ways the Lord has prepared you ahead of time. I could share with you example after example of how the Lord prepared us as a family before my sister's death. We didn't see it then, but looking back we can clearly see His hand. And it only confirms in our minds His sovereignty in every detail of our lives, even the small, seemingly insignificant details. He is always working in our lives to prepare the way before us, even when we cannot see it.

When my parents first moved to Florida, my sister was in her freshman year of high school. She made friends with a group of girls who she later found out were not headed in the same direction in life that she was. Their values were different. Their morals were different. The longer the relationships lasted, the more evident it became that Ginger needed to break them off and find a new group of friends. After about a year and a half, she did just that. But by doing so, she made some real enemies out of what had once been friends. They did not understand why she no longer wanted to go the places they went or do things they did.

Ginger was a starter on the high school basketball team. She loved playing basketball! Much like my older son, it didn't matter if her team was winning or losing, she would have a great big smile on her face and just absolutely loved playing the game! During her senior year of high school, she developed a severe case of asthma. After collapsing and nearly dying on the court, her coach, not wanting to take any more risks, left her sitting on the bench for the remainder of the season. Ginger graduated from high school with a real bitterness towards that coach because of the coach's decision to bench her.

A few weeks before the accident, Ginger called those girls who she had once been friends with and also called the coach she had played for. She met with each of them explaining her feelings and asking for forgiveness.

Nine days before the accident, Ginger bought a life insurance policy. How many eighteen-year-olds do you know who go out on their own and purchase life insurance? I don't know of any, except my sister. I get chills just thinking about this. The policy she purchased was for fifty thousand dollars, double indemnity. Double indemnity! Do you know what that means? That means if it's an accident the policy pays double. Ginger made one fifty-dollar payment on that policy.

On the night of the accident my parents gave Ginger her Christmas present, thirteen days early. They had no reason to, they just did. That night, my father, mother and sister had a special family dinner together for my father's birthday.

I believe God orchestrated each one of these events and caused them to happen just the way they did, to prepare us for what He knew was to come. You may think that these things were merely coincidences, but I could go on and on with examples of things that were clearly not coincidence. By the time I finished, you too would be convinced [if you're not already] as I am, that this was all part of His plan.

This was God's providential hand. In what seems to be little insignificant ways, He was preparing us and proving His compassion. Look at how He has prepared you in the past for this moment you are living today. And today, He is preparing you for what the future holds.

9 **Memorize God's Word.** Memorizing Scripture has always been a difficult thing for me, but that doesn't mean it's impossible! And it doesn't mean I shouldn't keep trying. You may have heard the old adage that says *anything worth having is worth working for*. Well, this is one thing that is, without a doubt, worth working for! When we are going through trials, tribulation, brokenness, what better thing to get us through than memorized scripture!?

I realized several years ago that when I really got serious about memorizing scripture, it became a whole lot easier. In a funny kind of way, I think it stretched my mind. It seemed the more I memorized, the easier it got. I believe it has actually improved my memory, and as I get older, this helps in other areas of my life as well!

I started with very simple verses like *Be still, and know that I am God* [Psalm 46:10a]. I wrote it on sticky notes and stuck them on the visor of my car, on my bathroom mirror, and on the refrigerator—where I go way too often. You will be amazed how easy it is to memorize a verse if you make yourself say it every time you open the refrigerator door!

It's a wonderful tool that will help heal your brokenness if you are able to pull those memorized bits of Scripture out of your mind's library when you need them. Another memorization aid is to put verses to music. Make up your own tunes. Sing Psalms of praise!

If ever I think I cannot memorize, I remind myself that in the third grade I, along with my classmates, memorized the entire chapter of Hebrews 11. If a third grader can memorize a whole chapter, we can memorize a verse! Memorized Scripture will help heal your brokenness.

10 Remember that God meant it for good!

In Genesis 50:19-20, Joseph both confronted and comforted his brothers, years after they sold him into slavery. This is what he said, *Do not fear, for am I in the place of God?* He was essentially saying to them *can I be the judge of this thing that you have done*? No, he could not.

Joseph realized that only God sees the big picture, and only God knows what is best for us. Can we be the judge of what God allows in our lives? Joseph goes on to say *as for you, you meant evil against me, but God meant it for good, to bring it about that many people should be kept alive as they are today*. His brothers meant evil towards Joseph when they carried out their plan to get rid of him, but God didn't. God meant it for good! And He used it for good in the lives of an entire nation and even beyond that. All the while, when Joseph's brothers were making their plans, they didn't know it, but God was planning to use their evil deeds for good *that many people should be kept alive*. He did just that. God used the brother's plans and Joseph's willing heart to save many people, even the brothers themselves.

Sometimes we think we know best about how things should work out. We think we know how things should fit together in the big puzzle of our lives—the circumstances and the timing. It all seems to be so clear to us, doesn't it?

I remember the story of a little boy who thought he was helping out by putting all the keys on a computer keyboard in alphabetical order. It makes me laugh when I think about it. Sometimes, we are like that little boy though. We want to put all the keys in the order that makes the most sense to us. But that's not always the order that is best for us.

Proverbs 3:5 says *Trust in the Lord with all your heart, and do not lean on your own understanding.*

I am also reminded of the story where another little boy was watching his mother create a beautiful tapestry. You've probably read or heard this story as well. The tapestry was stretched over a large wood frame and the boy sat beneath it on the floor, watching as his mother pushed and pulled the needle and threads back and forth through the fabric. From where the boy sat, he saw only the underside of the tapestry. It was matted with knots and pieces of different colored threads and was not very pretty to look at. The underside of the tapestry is similar to the view we have of our own lives.

But the mother, who sat above the tapestry looking down, sees a different picture. The picture she sees is one of beauty, as the character of the tapestry is being formed one thread at a time.

The little boy and the mother were both looking at the same tapestry, but with two different views. They each had a unique perspective. The mother could see character in the tapestry that the boy could not.

It's just like you and God, both looking at the tapestry of your life. You are both looking at the same life, but from different perspectives. The side you see looks like a matted, knotted-up, mess, with different lengths and colors of threads dangling all about. It may be filled with brokenness and a broken heart, trials, tribulations and burdens. But the side that God is looking at, looks like the character of a beautiful tapestry in the works.

Do you remember in the book of John, when Jesus was washing the feet of the disciples? When He came to Peter, Peter questioned Him, as he so often did. *He came to Simon Peter, who said to Him, Lord, do you wash my feet* [John 13:6]? And Jesus answered him in John 13:7: *What I am doing you do not understand now, but afterward you will understand.*

What He does in our lives and sometimes allows in our lives, we do not always understand. Even though we may not understand now, He promises we will someday.

Isaiah 55:8 says *For My thoughts are not your thoughts, neither are your ways My ways, declares the Lord.* His ways are perfect!

Psalm 18:30 says *This God—His way is perfect; the Word of the Lord proves true; He is a shield for all those who take refuge in Him.* He is a shield of protection and strength!

His thoughts are not my thoughts. His ways are not my ways. However, His way is perfect. We all need God's protection and His strength. We have to trust Him, and *be still, and know* that He is God!

The application:

1. Burdens give us opportunities
2. Burdens strengthen our prayer life
3. Burdens give us empathy
4. Burdens strengthen our testimony
5. Start an encouragement file
6. Add to someone's encouragement file
7. Beware of psychological effects
8. Look at how you've been prepared
9. Memorize scripture
10. Remember God meant it for good

I hope this book has been a help to you friend. I also hope that it helps you help others! That in turn will help you and it will glorify God.

I have listed the ten memory verses used in the chapters of this book at the end of the book and have created some cute coloring pages at the beginning of each chapter to help you with memorization. Feel free to tear those coloring pages out. Make copies of them. Place them on your bathroom mirror, and yes, on your refrigerator too, and anywhere else you frequent. Feel free to also share them with friends—they are my gift to you for completing this journey with me.

REFLECTION & APPLICATION

1. What did God teach me through this chapter?
2. How can I obediently respond to what I've learned?
3. What steps of faith does God want me to take now?

PRAYER & PETITIONS *Confession, Gratitude, Praise, and Requests*

MEDITATION & MEMORIZATION
Meditate on Psalm 1:1-3. Write out and memorize verse 2.

Epilogue

We have looked at the problem, the solution, and the applications. We talked about breaking down the wall of emotions, and we've seen the emotional difference between men and women. We found out that we cannot do this alone! We studied casting and bearing burdens and how God is the God of all comfort. We looked at growing in Christ and what it means to be a Christian. We talked about how much our response to burdens matters and the blessings of burdens. We discovered some practical applications. We reflected, prayed, meditated, and memorized. We've done all of this; now it is time for us to take action!

James 1:22 says *But be doers of the Word, and not hearers only, deceiving yourselves*. I had heard the first part of this verse many, many times, *be doers of the Word, and not hearers only*. However, I had never paid much attention to the last part of the verse, *and not hearers only, deceiving yourselves*.

The verse says that *hearers only*, people who only hear and do nothing about what they've heard [or read], are deceiving themselves. If all I do is hear or read, and I don't apply what I have learned, and I don't do what the Word of God tells me to do, I am deceiving myself! Could we be *hearers only* and be so deceived that we don't even realize it? I think we can.

Also, in James 4:17 we read *So, whoever knows the right thing to do and fails to do it, for him it is sin*. I could be deceiving my own self and committing sin, all at the same time.

It's as if there were a war going on inside of me, and there is! The Bible calls it the war of the flesh. My mind knows what to do. It has read it. It has heard it. It has studied it. Maybe it's even meditated on it and memorized it. But my will doesn't want to do it. It's a war alright! It's a battle of my emotions, my mind, and my will.

We must be diligent and consistent. We need to be faithful to continue to grow in Christ in spite of our brokenness. We have to break down the wall of emotions, remembering that every emotional response needs to be filtered through the Word of God. We should understand the emotional difference and remember that we cannot do it in our own strength, but only in His strength alone. Let's cast our burdens and be willing to bear the burdens of others. Let's remember that our response to burdens matters and recognize the blessings of burdens. And finally, let's allow the God of all comfort to have His will and His way in our lives.

Have you ever observed someone walking *up* a downward escalator? Just as that person walking up the downward escalator must keep moving to reach the top, we too must keep moving to reach the top. If we hesitate, if we look back, lack diligence or consistency or are not faithful, that downward escalator will very rapidly carry us down, down, down, even though, all along, we were heading in the right direction.

It is not enough just to be headed in the right direction. We must be headed in the right direction diligently, consistently, and faithfully. We must keep on keeping on and never, never, never, ever give up!

Jeremiah 31:3 is one of my favorite verses. It goes like this: *I have loved you with an everlasting love; therefore, I have continued My faithfulness to you.* In Hebrews 13:5 Jesus says *I will never leave you nor forsake you.*

Can you imagine a God Who loves us with an everlasting, eternal love? Can you trust a God Who draws us and will never, ever leave us or forsake us? What a wonderful and awesome God we serve! *Be still, and know that I am God* [Psalm 46:10a].

Verses

Be still, and know that I am God.
I will be exalted among the nations,
I will be exalted in the earth!
Psalm 46:10

When you pass through the waters, I will be with you;
and through the rivers, they shall not overwhelm you;
when you walk through fire you shall not be burned,
and the flame shall not consume you.
Isaiah 43:2

The steadfast love of the Lord never ceases;
His mercies never come to an end;
they are new every morning; great is your faithfulness.
Lamentations 3:22-23

Cast your burden on the Lord, and He will sustain you;
He will never permit the righteous to be moved.
Psalm 55:22

And let us not grow weary of doing good,
for in due season we will reap, if we do not give up.
Galatians 6:9

And the vessel he was making of clay was spoiled in the potter's hand,
and he reworked it into another vessel,
as it seemed good to the potter to do.
Jeremiah 18:4

Thus you will recognize them by their fruits.
Matthew 7:20

Not that I am speaking of being in need, for I have learned
in whatever situation I am to be content.
Philippians 4:11

The Lord upholds all who are falling and
raises up all who are bowed down.
Psalm 145:14

Blessed is the man [woman] who... delight[s] in
the law of the Lord, and... meditates day and night.
[S]he is like a tree planted by streams of water.
Psalm 1:1-3

We're building a worldwide online community of encouragers encouraging others
in the faith of Jesus Christ. So, grab a cup of coffee and *Join the movement*!

WWW.INSTAENCOURAGEMENTS.COM

www.facebook.com/InstaEncouragements

www.instagram.com/InstaEncouragements

www.pinterest.com/InstaEncourage

www.twitter.com/InstaEncourage

If you like hashtags as I do, please use #TheHeartThatHeals and/or #InstaEncouragements.

MISSION: Equipping you to be an encourager.

VERSE: *Therefore encourage one another and build one another up, just as you are doing* [1 Thessalonians 5:11].

VISION: To give followers the opportunity to daily encourage others in the faith and be the light in their little corner of the world.

PURPOSE: Our greatest purpose is to know Jesus Christ and to make Him known. It's really just that simple. We do that by presenting the Gospel of Jesus Christ in such a way that it turns non-Christians into converts, converts into disciples, and disciples into mature, fruitful leaders, who will in turn go into the world and reach others for Him.